# Ruby An

Down Home
Trailer Park Guide to

# Livin' Real Good

In Honor of
Queen Kelly
From
Those that know her

Other books by Ruby Ann Boxcar

*Ruby Ann's Down Home Trailer Park Cookbook*

*Ruby Ann's Down Home Trailer Park Holiday Cookbook*

*Ruby Ann's Down Home Trailer Park BBQin' Cookbook*

# Ruby Ann's

## Down Home Trailer Park Guide to

# Livin' Real Good

RUBY ANN BOXCAR

CITADEL PRESS
Kensington Publishing Corp.
www.kensingtonbooks.com

CITADEL PRESS books are published by

Kensington Publishing Corp.
850 Third Avenue
New York, NY 10022



All Kensington titles, imprints, and distributed lines are available at special quantity discounts for bulk purchases for sales promotions, premiums, fund-raising, educational, or institutional use. Special book excerpts or customized printings can also be created to fit specific needs. For details, write or phone the office of the Kensington special sales manager: Kensington Publishing Corp., 850 Third Avenue, New York, NY 10022, attn: Special Sales Department; phone: 1-800-221-2647.



Photos by Ruby Ann's husband, Dew



First printing: October 2003

10 9 8 7 6 5 4 3 2 1

Printed in the United States of America

Library of Congress Control Number 2003106144

ISBN 0-8065-2547-9

This here book is dedicated to my husband, Dew,
who's made me feel like I'm livin' good each
and every day durin' the past thirteen years
with his lovin' comments and his occasional
attempts to pick me up, even though the
doctors have all warned him again.

# Contents

*The guru of livin' real good and international queen of trailer park society, Ms. Ruby Ann Boxcar.*

# Preface: Hello Again from Ruby Ann

As I mentioned in *Ruby Ann's Down Home Trailer Park Cookbook,* all sorts of people are movin' into trailer parks, and now that me and my sister's books have been bringin' even more attention to and shinin' more light on this wonderful way of livin', the population in these parks is growin' beyond belief. That's why I decided to take pen to paper and write *Ruby Ann's Down Home Trailer Park Guide to Livin' Real Good.*

I'm sure that by now most of y'all have heard me referred to as a cross between Martha Stewart and Lulu from *Hee Haw.* Even though I don't understand the comparison of the latter, I take it as a compliment and I'd have to agree with the suggestion that me and Martha Stewart are somewhat alike. Just like Martha, I like to be creative with my decoratin', gardenin', entertainin', and money, as well. And I'm also pretty handy when it comes to crafts and helpful hints, as is she. But all you readers out there will be happy to know that when it comes to me personally buyin' stocks, the closest I get is stockin's, and, heck, those are just dang knee-highs, for goodness sakes. In any case, as you continue readin', y'all will find that I cross those tracks that even Martha never dared to cross, and I share my simple thoughts, ideas, creations, and just plain old ways of life that are sure to bring just as much inspiration and good-time fun as she has, in her own cardboard kind of way.

I'm sure my past three books have fleeced out any doubts that y'all might have had about the pleasures of livin' in a home with wheels. The only problem y'all have to face now is what all is expected from you by your neighbors. And even more than that, how can you add more delight and happiness to this already delightful life in a mobile abode. That's where my wonderful easy-to-read handbook comes in to play. Thanks to my selfless love and care for all my fans, friends, and fellow trailer dwellers, I've taken the time to make your life a lot easier. Unlike the many livin' out there in trailer parks across this great world of ours, you won't have to make all those embarrassin' first-time mistakes that they did. With this book you'll be sure to blend in—just like those gray hairs that you've taken your brown eyelash mascara to.

Now before we jump into the kinds of things that you're gonna find in this new book of mine, I want to warn all you loyal fans who've read the last three that the look and feel of this fourth one is gonna be a little different. For example, some of the chapters will be smaller in the amount of words that I use than others. Now that ain't 'cause I got lazy or nothin', but simply that unlike the other books in this series, I've actually added more illustrations. Y'all will still find the photo at the start of each chapter, which I know by the e-mails and such that I get from you, y'all love to see. But y'all will also find that in some of the chapters where I explain how to make something, I've included a set of illustrations that either my husband, Dew, has taken with his camera or my niece, Lulu Bell, has so graciously drawn to make the task easier. I hope that this new format is somethin' that each one of y'all finds helpful and even more fun.

And for those of y'all who've been livin' in trailers for years already, don't think that this book ain't got nothin' for you. Not only do I talk about how our new neighbors have more money than the last ones, but I throw a few ideas your way from my mobile home–minded way of thinkin' on how you can manage your own income regardless of what little there might be. And if that ain't enough, why I even let you in on some of my personal tricks to keep those dang neighborhood thugs from vandalizin' your lovely lawn statues. But don't think it ends right there. Goodness no! With fifteen chapters packed full of my trailer park knowledge, you're sure to learn somethin' new. And if nothin' else, you know that if you give this handbook as a housewarmin' present to those new neighbors that just moved in, they're sure to catch on quick to the methods and artful yard sculpturin' that you and others like you hold so dear.

Some of y'all, for one reason or another, haven't been able to take that plunge all the way into actually ownin' a trailer home, and that's all right. I know that you're kind of slowly workin' your way up the social ladder to mobile home owner one cinder block step at a time, and I totally understand. And not wantin' y'all to feel out of place, I've included a few things with step-by-step instructions that you can do yourselves to make your current brick-and-mortar home feel just like it has tires. Just one example of this would be where I help you to make your very own cigarette butt Christmas tree: There ain't nothin' like a fourteen-inch-tall Christmas tree made out of lipstick-stained cigarette butts and Styrofoam that'll fill your holidays with a feelin' that your home just might possibly blow away in a strong windstorm after all.

I know that some of y'all who have come to enjoy me and all the rest of the gang at the High Chaparral Trailer Park have been wonderin' just what's been goin' on in our lives. Well, y'all are in luck. Just like always, I give you an insightful insider's look and update on every little thing that's taken place since my BBQ book came out. So get your prayer chain buddies on the phone, 'cause y'all are goin' to be spendin' hours askin' for tons of divine intercedin' for my poor neighbors and family members who reside in all twenty lots of the High Chaparral.

Oh, and one more quick thing. I've ended each chapter with a question that one of my many admirers has e-mailed me in the past. And as you would expect, each of these questions, which I've painstakin'ly taken the time to answer, is related to that chapter that it's in.

I know that there are others out there in this happy trailer park world of ours who could probably give you advice and tips on all these topics that I'm gonna talk about in this here book, but for some reason or another, y'all seem to trust me. Y'all know I ain't out to hurt no one or make a fool out of my readers. Plus y'all know that I happen to love trailer park livin'. And y'all just feel plain old at ease with me. That's the way it's been all my life. For some odd reason people always love to come to me when they have questions about life in general, and I feel that the good Lord has blessed me with the answers. Yes, dear reader, it is up to me to do all I can to help you live a more glorious and prosperous life. And I do love it. It's like my Pa-Pa used to say, "Ruby Ann, you've always got a thought for every word." I wish he was still alive today just so I could ask him what the heck he meant by that statement.

So, dear reader, without any further ado, let's grab that pencil, pen, or yellow highlighter and join me, your guru of the double wide, as we get crackin' into the wonderful world of trailer park livin'.

Update

# The Residents of the High Chaparral Trailer Park, Lot by Lot

*Despite the pig farm next door, the business at the newly opened Rinky Dink Roller Rink is boomin'.*

On behalf of the good folks at the High Chaparral Trailer Park, I'd like to bid you a warm heartfelt hello. As you can imagine, with all that's goin' on with me and my sister, everybody has been keepin' real busy since I last gave you the trailer park residential update in my BBQ cookbook. Why, it seems like this just might be the best year that we've ever had up here at the trailer park. I say that on account of the recent good news that we just got. It seems that the property value is gonna jack on up here in the next year on account of some plans that the state and county have decided upon, which in turn affects us. Thanks to those fine folks in Little Rock, the High Chaparral will soon be waterfront property. That's right! You heard me correct. Come August of next year we're gonna be able to step outside of our trailers, walk about one hundred feet, and sunbathe or picnic right next to our own lagoon. Who'd have ever thought? Why, Dottie Lamb has already placed an order for beach chairs and other assorted outdoor water items for the Lamb's Super Store just to keep up with the demand that we've already put on her. Sure it might be cold outside right now, but once the state gets that infrastructure built (around June or August), we'll be ready to enjoy our new aquatic lives. Plus it always is hard for us folks to have money and not spend it. Oh, I forgot to tell you that on top of all this wonderful news from the state, they've turned around and given all of us residents a cash amount just for lettin' 'em build this waterway so close to our homes. Needless to say, we was more than happy to take their money, and we did it with a smile to boot. So if you happen to make it up this way next summer, make sure you stop by, and bring your swimsuit. After all, the state's largest wastewater (whatever that is) recycling plant will be open to both us folks at the High Chaparral as well as the general public. And don't worry if you forget your sunscreen, 'cause the good Lord knows Connie Kay, our local Avon, Mary Kay, Shaklee, and Amway distributor (just to name a few of her franchises) is always well stocked when it comes to sun-protectin' skin products.

Since my last report, lots of stuff has been happenin'. We had one of the pillars of our community move out and another stripper has moved in, bringin' the number of exotic dancers to a whoppin' total of six, if you count the newly semi-retired Vance, Harry, and Elroy over in Lot #19. My sister is actin' odd. Her rival Faye Faye has been playin' around with her recently discovered talents, and Faye Faye's daughter's hotel is doin' even better than before. Why, you won't believe the big heart Opal has got, or the good news my niece, Lulu Bell, received. In any case, lots of stuff has happened since we been apart, so hold on to your chair as we see what's been happenin' to the folks at the High Chaparral Trailer Park, lot by lot!

## Lot #1

Opal Lamb-Inman and her husband, Dick Inman, are doin' just fine, and are still in love. Yes, many of us thought their relationship would never last on account of the fact that Opal is just dog-ugly and Dick has his sight, but they've proved us wrong by markin' their one-year anniversary this past September. Actually the anniversary was marked a little earlier in the month on account of conflicts that the two had on their actual anniversary day. You see, Dick, whose new law office is just goin' like gangbusters, wanted to do somethin' special for Opal for their first-year anniversary, so he hunted and searched the Internet tryin' to find the perfect getaway vacation for 'em. He would have used our local travel agent Vonda Peters, but her company, Travel Unlimited, only books airfare, car rentals, motels, and all-inclusive vacation packages for travel inside the great state of Arkansas. Vonda don't want the pressures that out-of-state travel bookin' can cause for a travel agent, plus she likes it just the way it is. She is, however, addin' bus travel reservations to her list of services come 2004, but as you might have guessed, that will only cover routes inside the state.

Anyways, Dick managed to find tickets to Athens, Greece, for a fantastic price. Why, he was gonna pamper Opal to the point that she'd feel like a princess by bringin' along their nineteen- and twenty-year-old male maid and butler, Uri Krochichin and Buck N. Hiney. That way she wouldn't have to lift a finger and could just have fun. Unfortunately the prices were only good for a certain week in late September, which happened to fall on the exact dates that Opal's momma, Dottie Lamb, and her roommate and recently widowed High Chaparral Trailer Park manager, Ben Beaver, had already set aside for their trip to Walt Disney World. Both Opal and Dottie couldn't possibly be gone on the same dates, since one of 'em had to manage their growin' business at Lamb's Super Store. Since Dottie and Ben's tickets were nonrefundable, there was no question as to who would go and who would stay. It looked like Dick's plans for a Greece getaway would just have to wait until next year, but Opal would have no part of that. Bein' the kind soul that she is, she told Dick to go ahead and go without her. Well, Dick told her straight out that there was no way he was goin' without her or at least, I should say, not alone. Opal told him he didn't have to go alone, but should go on ahead and take Uri and Buck with him. Knowin' that you never say no to Opal, Dick and the boys headed off on the trip that they self-titled "Greece Through the Back Door," whatever that means. Opal said it's got to do with savin' money or some such thing. Sister Bertha asked Opal if she could trust her husband with all them "foreign women runnin' around over there in next to nothin'." Of course Opal set Sister Bertha straight and told her that Dick ain't like that. Why, accordin' to her, the only time Dick ever looks at another woman is to make comments about her hair or sense of fashion. No, he's devoted to only one woman, and that is dear, sweet Opal Lamb-Inman. As a matter of fact, Dick is so devoted that when him and his male servants would go out durin' the day, he'd wear a 5- x 7-inch photo of Opal around his neck just to remember her durin' their anniversary. He did add that it tended to keep the usually pushy peddlers sellin' trinkets away from him, and he did notice that for some reason a lot more flies were attracted to him than the others on the trip.

## Lot #2

As most of y'all will recall Anita Biggon's business, the Three Cigarettes in the Ashtray Bar, burnt to the ground and she relocated her new place, Anita's Bar and Grill, down by the highway. And you might recall that she even added a drive-thru that was protected by large trees, makin' it acceptable for anyone who had a hankerin' for some of that place's wonderful food to drive right up and get it without talk of scandal. Well, business has been so good that Anita decided to revamp the inside and put everything on wheels. Thanks to movable interior walls and slidin' partitions, every weekday at 11:30 A.M. Anita's Bar and Grill becomes Anita's Café. Of course, she still serves drinks for all the regular customers, but you have to use the back door to get in. Durin' the day the front door takes you right in the café, where Anita has even turned the pool tables into all-you-can-eat food buffets by simply puttin' a piece of plywood across 'em and installin' tannin' bed lights in the hangin' lamps above. And she's even gotten kind of fancy by addin' a little table where you can deep-fry your own pickle. I tell you, with them movin' walls and all, she's got that place so slick that, even the best Baptist could go in there for a bite at lunchtime without feelin' guilty. Of course, come 1:30 in the afternoon the place changes back into a den of sin until the next afternoon when hunger hits and the lunch crowd arrives.

## Lot #3

The last I heard, Hubert and Lois Bunch's businesses, includin' the original Taco Tackle Shack, Taco Tackle Shack North, and their drive-thru hut the Fisherman's Friend was all doin' just great. As y'all will recall, I told you in my BBQ book how they'd added the cliff divers/midgets jumpin' from chairs into turtle pools to their Taco Tackle Shack North location on Wednesday and Thursday nights in an attempt to drum up business. Well, needless to say, business is still boomin' at that store on them nights. And don't quote me on this, but a little birdie told me that they've recently seen the Bunches over at Lamb's Super Store lookin' at new turtle pools. I can't help but wonder if we're gonna be seein' shows at the original Taco Tackle Shack as well in the not-too-distant future. Of course neither Lois or Hubert for that matter will comment on that bit of news, not even to me. What they will say is that there is gonna be some change in the air, but that's it. Of course I can't help but wonder if that change has anything to do with the dinner show itself. After all, last August, when the divers who've been performin' all this time went on vacation, the Bunches where forced to make some changes in their water show. Since the actual amount of midget residents in this area is slim, Lois and Hubert had to revamp the whole

Wednesday and Thursday program entirely. Durin' those two weeks that their divers were off baskin' in the sun, the twice-a-week Taco Tackle Shack North's show consisted of two blindfolded chihuahuas on water skis bein' pulled by a poodle back and forth down a slip-n-slide. The chihuahuas would jump through hoops and do tricks and maneuvers that would've easily challenged even them trick water-skiers down at Cypress Gardens. And for their big finale, right after the aqua ballet routine performed to musical selections from the opera *Carmen,* them little chihuahuas take off down that slip-n-slide and onto a ramp where they fly across the dinin' room and into the open minnow tank by the tackle and fish gear part of the store. I tell you, every Wednesday and Thursday night like clockwork when them pooches would land in that minnow tank the crowds would leap to their feet in applause. And you could tell that them little dogs just loved to do it three times a night. Of course the Bunches loved it as well. Not only did they have happy customers, but they was also rackin' in the big bucks. And when you consider that the dogs are workin' for kibble, well, you can imagine the worry that them poor cliff-divin' midgets must have felt when they came back only to be told to take another two weeks off while the skiin' chihuahuas were held over. Sure the cliff divers are back, but I'm sure they can't help but wonder for just how long.

## Lot #4

Nellie Tinkle, her husband, C.M., and their roommate, Wendy Bottom, are doin' just fine. C.M. is still enjoyin' retirement, and Wendy and Nellie are now tradin' off on their organ duties at the Holier Than Most Baptist Church where we all attend (Nellie does Sunday mornin' services while Wendy with her one-finger style of playin' covers the Wednesday and Sunday-night services). And of course, Nellie is still enjoyin' her by-appointment-only pipe cleanin' business, Nellie's Tinklin' Organ. But nowadays, as I mentioned in my last book, Nellie has been real busy in the evenin' workin' down at the new Rinky Dink Roller Rink.

Even though she complains about the terrible heat that the onetime barn manages to have durin' the Arkansas summer months, she still loves to work that skatin' rink organ like there was no tomorrow. To be honest, Harland says he's doin' the best he can to cool the place down so Nellie ain't so miserable. One of the things that he does do is to open that big barn door that they decided to keep up by the front. Back when Harland bought the worndown barn with the money he got from that bowlin'-ball-to-the-head accident, he found out that it was gonna cost more to replace the barn door with a new wall and a regular entrance than it would to just refurbish the original door. So he went along with the construction manager and kept the door there. And to be honest, when that massive barn door is opened they do get a real nice cool breeze that comes off the pond outside. The only problem is that the Rinky Dink is right next to a workin' hog farm, so the pond that I mentioned is actually the hog pond, which ain't all that great when it comes to smells. Sure the light wind cools down the place, but when they got that door opened up the concession stand sales drop like a lead balloon.

Gettin' back to Nellie, for the first time in her life she's got quite the new fan base. Why, even the younger crowd treats her like she was some kind of a celebrity. With the way they act toward her, askin' for her autograph and such, you'd think she was Ann Murray or Helen Reddy or some other big rock star. They just love the way she plays that organ. Personally I think it's the way she takes them songs and pieces 'em together. You see, Nellie has this God-given talent of puttin' together medleys, which before could only be heard durin' a Sunday service at the Holier Than Most Baptist Church. Well now she's also used it at the Rinky Dink. You should hear the arrangement that she made from a few Madonna songs and turned into a good eight-minute skate. When she starts up that KC and the Sunshine Band Medley, my husband, Dew, is the first to hit the floor, with me followin' close behind. I tell you, when she pumps one of these out it's just like magic on the floor. An example of this took place just last August when regardless of the 105-degree heat wave we was havin', she managed to whip that skatin' crowd into a lightnin'-fast frenzy with her new Billy Ray Cyrus medley. Why, my own niece, Lulu Bell, who as y'all will recall is Billy Ray's number one fan in the world, was so excited that she grabbed her boyfriend/fiancé, Billy Bob Buttons, and start a dang crack-the-whip skate right there in the middle of the floor. Before Nellie could get to the chorus of "Achy Breaky Heart" everybody had joined in, with Dottie Lamb and Ben Beaver, who skates while seated in his wheelchair, makin' up the rear. A good time was had by all. Well, that was until the whip finally cracked and Ben Beaver, wheelchair and all, went flyin' across the rink, through the rail, where he managed to take out Opal Lamb and Wendy Bottom, and then finally out the open barn door. The bench that Opal and

Wendy had been seated on flipped over upon impact and landed in a way that made it turn into some kind of crazy freakish catapultin' ramp, propellin' Ben, Opal, and Wendy into the air. As you can guess, poor old Opal and dear, sweet Wendy ended up headfirst in the hog pond. I tell you, though, if there'd been an East German judge at the rink that day, she'd have given both those gals a 9.6 for those dives and aerial maneuvers. As for Ben, not only did he clear the hog pond, but he also managed to jump two Suburbans, a Schwan's truck, and Donna Sue's Bonneville, which had broken down on her way to the rink, finally landin' in the neighborin' henhouse. You should have seen the feathers fly. Amazingly he survived the whole ordeal without a scratch. As for the chickens, well, they didn't lay anythin' but scrambled eggs for a week after that. Of course no one tried to sue Harland or the Rinky Dink. After all, what jury or judge could possibly decide in Ben's favor once they'd heard Nellie's hypnotic rhythms on the organ? Plus Harland gave Ben a whole two months' worth of free rentals on his roller skates.

## Lot #5

Momma and Daddy are doin' great over in Lot #5, and I'm glad to report that Daddy has finally given up on that horrid toupee he was wearin'. He woke up one mornin' to find a optically challenged squirrel doin' the dance of love with it on the dresser. When Daddy tried to swipe the little fella's new love doll away, it just grabbed hold of that matted synthetic hairpiece and took off across the room and out the open window, leavin' nothin' behind but a trail of dust and some nuts up on the dresser. Personally I think Daddy looks much better. He don't talk about his toupee, but I think he kind of misses it. Whenever a Bert Reynolds flick comes on I notice Daddy gets a little teary eyed.

Nowadays you'll find Daddy down at Lamb's Super Store, where he works as a greeter. He's been there for four weeks now even though his job has slightly changed from when he first started. When you'd come in he'd greet you and give you a buggy, but now he ain't allowed to touch the buggies. It seemed that before he'd let you start pushin' one of those carts through the store he'd adjust the wheels to make sure your cart was in top shape for your shoppin' experience. This sounded like a nice thing to do, but Daddy had folks backed all the way out to the parkin' lot waitin' to get in. Most folks just skipped the buggies all together and carried their merchandise around the store in their arms. Of course this led to talk about lawsuits for back problems and possible hernias. Daddy's job description was quickly changed.

Momma, who got tired to stayin' around the trailer by herself at night when Daddy worked, decided to get a part-time job of her own. She now works as a pizza delivery driver for Papa Lamb's Pizza. Of course the only problem with this whole thing is that since Momma don't know how to drive, she has to hire a taxi to run her to each house so she can make her deliveries. With the excellent tips and the $2.25 an hour wage that she makes, she brings home around $1.37 a week after taxes and taxis.

## Lot #6

As y'all know if you've been readin' my past three books, my older sister, Donna Sue, who lives in Lot #6, is a stripper as well as the headliner over at the Blue Whale Strip Club. And as y'all also know, in the past she's happened to be quite the hot item amongst those who'd come out to see her dance. Now, I ain't sayin' she's got a bad reputation, but she has made Mae West look like a saint. Let's just say that there have been times over the years that she's given McDonald's a run for their money when it comes to the amount of folks served, if you catch my drift. But here lately with the success of her book *Donna Sue's Down Home Trailer Park Bartending Guide*, she has been attractin' more of the big Hollywood types to the Blue Whale. Why, you name a male star and most likely he's been there to see her dance. I myself think these Hollywood visits are more like how you drive by a little slower when you pass a car wreck type of experience for these fellas than a personal thrill type thin'. Of course, havin' a celebrity in the audience ain't all that new to Donna Sue when she dances. If she had a dollar for every time she took change from Ernest Borgnine or a bowl of Quaker Oats from Wilford Brimley she'd be rich. But my sister will also be the first to tell you that she ain't never taken none of them stars to her trailer. Oh no, she can't afford to get into the tabloids. After all, that might interfere with her probation.

Here lately my sister has made an about-face. Sure she's still dancin', but she's curtailed her carousin' to just one man, and what a man he is. Seventy-four-year-old Buford Pits not only happens to be the king of the watermelon stands in all of Arkansas, with eleven just between the High Chaparral and the fifty-mile drive to Little Rock, but he also happens to be my sister's steady beau. And I'll tell you, they seem to hit it off pretty good. Buford, who regardless of what time of day it might be, is always known for his dapper wardrobe, which usually consists of a golf shirt, a pair of tux pants, and suspenders, also bathes on a regular basis as well, which is a first for my sister's datin' pool. Of course, bein' a big-business tycoon like he is, you know he's got class, and if you don't know it, then his orderin' of a Manhattan with a shot of peppermint schnapps every time he's near a bar is sure to help you catch on.

One of Buford's favorite things to do on a date is ballroom dancin'. Of course with his bad hip and such my sister always does all the leadin' and dippin', which really is somethin' to behold. But needless to say, with Donna Sue's dancin' skills and Buford's loose dentures, they are quite the couple on the dance floor.

When watermelon season is over and the cold weather starts to move in, old Buford turns his roadside stands into Christmas tree lots where folks can come and pick up a fern to take home and decorate for the holidays. Of course, Donna Sue has assured me that she ain't gonna let her new boyfriend give her one of his trees for Christmas. She ain't that kind of a person who would take advantage of a relationship regardless of who her boyfriend is. No, instead she's gonna get her Christmas tree just like everybody else around here does. She's gonna drive up to one of Buford's tree stands after hours with her car lights off and steal one.

## Lot #7

Our beloved Pastor Ida May Bee has been really busy with the church. Since she don't drive, her husband/song service leader and former bus driver, Brother Woody Bee, takes her to all her appointments around the surroundin' areas of the state. As y'all know, last year we gave Pastor Ida May Bee a portable computer for her car, which she uses while on the road. And since she ain't got one at work, she also uses it at home. As I said in my BBQ book, the massive computer part is in her trunk so it's only mobile if it's in the car. This means that Pastor Ida May Bee has to have Brother Woody Bee pull the car up next to her bedroom window, so she can run a phone line from the trailer to the computer out in the trunk. Well, as you might have guessed, Pastor Ida has really taken to the Internet, and in a good way. She's managed to turn our church page into somethin' that few of us would have ever thought possible. In just a matter of months Pastor Ida May was able to turn the Internet highway, which is layered with porn and scams, into the Internet highway to heaven *all by herself.* Not only does our church Web site talk about what we believe, give some inspirational thoughts, and directions to our church as well as times of services, but, thanks to Pastor Ida May Bee, you can now engage in religious activities online as well. Like a beacon in the night, she offers her services to all those lost souls in need via their DSL High Speed Connection or dial up modem. For example, if you've already preordered from our congregation's online store and received in the mail your one-servin' Communion kit, which comes complete with a disposable grape juice box and jalapeño cheese–flavored Communion cracker, then you can simply pay a small fee to download an Mp3 of Pastor Ida May Bee. In the download she conducts a Communion service and includes a selection of beeps to indicate when you're to drink your juice box and cheesy cracker. She also offers online weddin' and funeral services to the religious Web surfers. And until recently you could even do a virtual altar call, which was followed by an in-home baptismal. All you did was click on the virtual altar and your little cartoon person would get up out of the pew and walk down to the front for prayer. At that time you'd enter your credit card or PayPal account number, then you'd be instructed to go and run your bath, say your prayer, dive in, and finally, after your credit card was accepted, you'd hear Pastor Ida May Bee's voice instruct you on when to dunk yourself. Currently, however, she's put a hold on this service after one of the online users nearly electrocuted himself when his laptop accidentally fell into the bathtub. Pastor Ida May Bee was just devastated over the whole thing and might just close down the entire site altogether, even though its income has helped to pad the budget durin' these hard economical times. But it was Sister Bertha of Lot #12 who reminded us that at least if this here fella had passed on to glory, he'd have gone there as a Baptist.

## Lot #8

You should have seen my niece, Lulu Bell's face when she got the papers from the state sayin' that both she and her somewhat challenged boyfriend Billy Bob Buttons could legally be married. Since both of 'em are lick short of a sealed envelope, they had to get permission to join in holy matrimony. Why, even Billy Bob refused to spend the night in Lulu

Bell's trailer until the state said he could be her mister. Of course, anyone around these parts could have told the state that both Lulu Bell and Billy Bob would be just fine together—after all, look at what they've done on their own. Lulu Bell has been a regular Donald Trump when it comes to the way she's been handlin' all them properties her late daddy left her. And she's turned the pool hall she owns into a thrivin' business all by herself. And as for Billy Bob, well his Suck and Squirt Car Wash is doin' great business and there's even been talk about openin' one up in both Conway and Perryville. As far as a weddin' day goes, the kids ain't set one yet, but they did go ahead and decide on the dates for their bachelor and bachelorette parties, which was just this past October.

Lulu Bell invited all us ladies at the High Chaparral to attend, and since her no-good momma had skipped out of her life many years back leavin' all us gals in the community to raise her, we couldn't help but say yes. Even Pastor Ida May Bee agreed to attend the gatherin', which was to be held on a Monday night at the original Taco Tackle Shack. Lulu Bell had made all the arrangements for her party, so we had fruit cups, them little wienies in a cheese dip, and finger sandwiches. And for entertainment, Vance Poole and his Beef Stick Boys showed up with their boom box and stripped for us. Lulu Bell had a good time. Later when asked, Pastor Ida May Bee said that she thought the little wienies were pretty good.

The followin' night Billy Bob held his bachelor party at the Blue Whale Strip Club, which had closed just for the event. He, too, served little wienies in a cheese sauce, along with a fruit cup, and finger sandwiches. And not to be outdone by his future wife, Billy Bob also had strippers, but I believe Vance Poole and his Beef Stick Boys danced to different songs than they had the night before. My husband, Dew, who was in attendance, said that he was not impressed at all with the little wienies or the cheese for that matter.

## Lot #9

Good news, Harland's head has shrunk back to its normal size, and with the exception of him not bein' able to see things in color with his left eye, he seems to be doin' just fine after that bowlin'-ball-to-the-head incident. His wife, Juanita, had to curtail her hours at the Piggly Wiggly on account of how busy she's been with the new business she and her husband started. Why, Juanita has even had to cut the time she spent drivin' the local bookmobile in half, which means it runs on the first Saturday of each month from 10:00 A.M. to 10:15 A.M.

And speakin' of Harland and Juanita's new business, the Rinky Dink Roller Rink is doin' just great. Well, that is, except for the water problem they were havin'. You see, the Rinky Dink, as I've stated before, is in an old barn located right next to a hog pond. And with the water table that the piece of property has, when the first rain comes, the roller rink fills up with water. Well, Harland had a special pump and water runoff put in outside the rink, which stopped the floodin' of the floor, but durin' a bad cold spell this September it froze up. The poor rink got flooded and frozen as well. Not bein' quitters, Juanita and Harland, who by then was finally able to walk on his own, took what some would call a lemon and turned it into lemon pie by offerin' ice skatin' instead. And just in the past few months, it's become so popular that there's even been talk down at the high school of startin' up our very own hockey team. Of course, I don't think that's gonna pan out since we'd have to ship the kids off to Minnesota in order for them to play another school. The good part about the whole thing is that Harland and Juanita Hix and their little girls, Harlinda and Bonita, are finally doin' well both physically and monetarily. Lord knows it's about time. I tell you, them poor folks had been about as unlucky as one of my sister's boyfriends.

## Lot #10

And now for somethin' just terrible. With the recent economical crisis and the fact that the Republicans are in office, our school budgets have been drastically cut back. It looks like we completely misunderstood the whole political idea of "no child left behind." I think what they was sayin' was that no child will be left behind when it comes to the effects of educational cuts. In any case, the first thing to go was our school cafeteria program. Since the government says that the school still has to serve your kids a hot meal, they still got a cafeteria staff, but it consists of Molly Piper, who I told y'all about in my BBQ book. Yes, dear reader, they had to let dear old Ollie White of Lot #10 go. So now all them poor kids get at lunchtime is a choice of chicken pot pies or beef pot pies, which Molly sticks in the microwave and nukes for five minutes. Why, 'cause of the cutbacks and the thinnin' out of the staff, even the annual

Hairnet Award for outstandin' cookin' in a school lunch program has been canceled indefinitely, or at least until the next election.

But don't feel bad for Ollie, because at the age of sixty-five she's started a new career. The old days of cookin' for a bunch of heartless, snot-nosed little brats are long gone for Ollie White. Now she is the head sample lady at Lamb's Super Store. When it comes to free bites of toothpicked breakfast links, tiny drinks of frozen orange juice, little slivers of pizza rolls, or even the ever-popular cocktail wienie in the latest bottled BBQ sauce, the buck stops with Ollie White. With her new postin', nothin' can be sampled on the floor of Lamb's Super Store without Ollie's say-so. And in an attempt to draw new customers she's really taken this whole samplin' thing to a new level. She still does the traditional tester portions, but she's also added to that list samples of motor oil, baby wipes, ice-meltin' salt, garden fertilizer, fish food, bath soap, and assorted laxatives. Now, that's progress for you. Ollie is content with her new job and plans on holdin' it for as long as they need her or until things change back at the school, which reminds me, Ollie asks that you please vote Democrat come the next elections.

## Lot #11

Kyle Chitwood of Lot #11 is glad to be workin' back behind the bar again servin' drinks at Anita's Bar and Grill. He's also taken on the job of host for their "Kickin' Karaoke Night," which is every Monday except durin' football season. Of course nobody goes no more on account of the fact that my niece, Lulu Bell, and her boyfriend hog the dang mike all night long. For some reason they think they're the next Kathie Lee Gifford and Billy Ray Cyrus, and I guess I got to admit, they might just be right. After all, neither Lulu Bell or Billy Bob can sing. Personally I think they're more along the lines of Kid Rock and Pamela Anderson, but that's just me.

Kyle's wife, Kitty Chitwood, has recently made a new addition to Gas and Smokes. She's added a tannin' facility to the ever-popular convenience store, and accordin' to several folks around this part of the woods, it's about time this modern-day miracle finally reached us. Actually it's just one bed, which she's put over between the Ms. Pac-Man machine and the Bionic Woman pinball game. There's been talk about adding an additional bed because of the demand, though Kitty won't comment on it. Mum's the word on this subject—but I think she's gonna do it. After all, she just recently pulled out both the Space Invaders arcade and the Frogger machine. I think Momma has started tannin'. I could be wrong, but I say this 'cause the folks who do use Kitty's tannin' bed come out lookin like a zebra on account of the fact that Kitty don't change the bulbs. Sure, she bought extras, but she rents the bulbs out to Anita to keep the all-you-can-eat lunch buffet hot. Still, I got to hand it to Kitty for at least thinkin' outside of the box and bringin' in somethin' new. If people keep thinkin' like she does, it won't be more than another ten or twelve years till we're likely to get a chiropractor in here.

## Lot #12

I warned y'all that self-righteous Bible thumpin' Sister Bertha of Lot #12 was gonna try and buy the *Pangburn Bugle* when our old trailer park neighbors and good friends Lovie and Elmer Birch put it up for sale just before movin' out of town, and I was right. Luckily, however, bein' the tightwad that she is, she put in what would be considered a very low bid durin' the silent auction, even though she's got more money than King Midas had gold. The bad part was that even her low bid was more than anyone else had put up, and it appeared that the *Pangburn Bugle* would soon be heraldin' her own personal thoughts, notions on who is sinnin' and who ain't, and just tons of personal lectures that, to be honest with you, none of us cared to read with our RC Colas in the mornin'. But as fate would have it (or divine intervention as Pastor Ida May Bee likes to discreetly put it), at the last minute the tables on the paper turned. My darlin' mother-in-law Momma Ballzak in a drunken stupor while attemptin' to buy a personal ad in the paper's lonely hearts section somehow managed to place a bid that was higher than Sister Bertha's. Momma's bid came in just minutes before the auction was to come to an end. In fairness, which sums up the Birches to a tee, they tried to contact Sister Bertha at her trailer to inform her of the new bid, but since she was out observin' other people with her neighborhood watch committee for sin, she missed the call. You should have seen her face when she found out that the *Pangburn Bugle* had slipped through her hands, and when she found out that the difference between her bid and Momma Ballzak's was a difference of 7¢, well, let's just say, she wasn't happy. Of course, Pastor Ida May Bee likes to point out the number seven is God's number.

Since then Sister Bertha has done somethin' that none of us ever thought we'd see her do. She actually invested in my sister, Donna Sue's food business. Those of you who've read Donna Sue's bartendin' guide already know that she recently started up yet another business endeavor, this one bein' a hot dog/warm roasted nuts stand that you hook up to your car and pull around from place to place. And for some reason Sister Bertha wanted a piece of the franchise. Well, not bein' one to turn money down regardless of whose it might be, Donna Sue accepted, and within less than three hours Sister Bertha had her very own Wienies on Wheels. The only thing that she did change was the optional warm nuts part of the business, 'cause she thought it was just a little too spicy for her clientele down at the Flea Bath Flea Market over by Heber Springs. Instead she's givin' the cart her own little flair by usin' the warm nut portion of the cart as a container for her own line of desserts, Sister Bertha's Sent From Above Ambrosia Salad. And in an attempt to separate her Wienies on Wheels from the other Wienies on Wheels franchises, which are currently owned by my sister's coworkers at the Blue Whale Strip Club, Sister Bertha prays over every sale as it happens as well as takes time to personally anoint your wienie. Don't worry, she wears them disposable plastic gloves.

## Lot #13

You know, folks, the answer to the question about whether Mickey Ray Kay would leave the job he loved with the wonderful folks at the Dr Pepper plant to go and work over at Lamb's Sodas for a heck of a lot more money was just a matter of time. I mean, sure, Mickey Ray thought the world of his coworkers and even to this day he'll be the first to tell you how great Dr Pepper is (like we need somebody to tell us that), but how do you turn down a job that'd start you off at double your current salary, pays 100 percent of your insurance, lets you take off for four weeks with paid vacation every year, and gives you a newly restored custom-painted Byzantine Gold 1970 Cadillac Fleetwood Seventy-five Sedan with a recently installed Medium Gold Dorian cloth interior and Sierra grain vinyl trim to call your very own? Heck, I'd even promote Tab for that kind of a deal! No, we all knew Mickey Ray was gonna have to switch. He'd have been a full-blown idiot if he hadn't. So this past Monday, May 26, at 5:07 P.M., Mickey Ray Kay took his time card and punched out, popped open a can of Dr Pepper, and with tears in every one of his co-worker's eyes, he walked out of the bottlin' company for the very last time on the exact day that he'd started workin' for that upstandin' company just twenty-two years earlier. As far as his new job goes, Mickey Ray says it's good. It's a new challenge for him, tryin' to get a brand-new soda company up and runnin' with the big boys so to speak. And as for the perks, well, Mickey Ray says he can't complain even though he's already had to change the alternator, install a brand-new radiator, and replace most of the electrical wirin' inside that car.

You'd have thought that Connie Kay would've slowed down now that Mickey Ray is bringin' all that extra money home, but oh no, far be it from her to take a pill and catch her breath. She's still peddlin' her Tupperware, Amway, Shacklee, Avon, and Mary Kay from door to door. And she's just recently stepped out into a brand new endeavor as well. Just this past July, before Mickey Ray left his old job, Connie Kay took out a lease on one of the storefronts that my niece, Lulu Bell, owns, and she opened up a brand new Merle Norman Cosmetics. Needless to say, we was all agasp. Who'd have ever thought Merle Norman would actually make its way to this part of the state? As you can imagine, we are just thrilled, but I don't know how Connie does it, spreadin' herself so thin like that. I guess all we can do is keep her in our prayers, and just hope she don't go loopy on us anytime in the near future. Of course, I tell y'all, I really wish Connie would become a sales rep for Kirby. The good Lord knows I sure could use a new high-quality vacuum cleaner on my shag carpetin'. I laid down on the floor yesterday to do some light exercises and fell asleep. When I woke up from that unplanned nap I had little tiny pieces of potato chips, pretzels, and a couple of raisins stuck on the side of my face. Why, we don't even eat raisins.

Wanda Kay, Mickey Ray's momma, gave up her booth at the Flea Bath Flea Market on account of how when she was away gettin' herself a Diet-Rite from the concession stand, somebody accidentally knocked her photo imagin' transfer equipment on the floor, breakin' it into thousands of little pieces. At first Wanda thought she might be able to put it back together, but when I jumped on it, I mean, when it fell off the table and naturally broke into that many tiny pieces, it was clear that she wouldn't be printin' off any more of them off-center discolored T-shirts, calendars, or coffee mugs ever again. Of course, it was all for the best.

Her misfortune at the flea market made a way for her to go and work with her daughter-in-law down at the new store. And as you can imagine, Connie was more than happy to have some help. At first she was only openin' the store on Friday and Saturdays, which gave her plenty of time to deliver and sell all her other lines of products durin' the rest of the week. So what she'd do come Friday mornin' is give Wanda a complete makeover on just the left side of her face with Merle Norman Cosmetics and let her set up in the front window of the store so people walkin' by could see the big difference that it made. And it worked. I tell you, Wanda looked twenty years younger. Why, I bet it'd be safe to say that she'd have looked forty years younger if she'd had the right side of her face done as well. Needless to say, Wanda's window display was bringin' folks in. And the good thing was that she could just set up there in a chair and read magazines, sip on a Diet-Rite, and take it easy. It sounded like the perfect job. Of course as the summer drew on, and the temperature started risin', this cushy way of makin' a livin' started to heat up a bit. Long story short, Connie finally had to take Wanda out of the window on account of heat stroke. Plus with the way she was sweatin' like a pig, even the good side of her face was startin' to resemble a wax figure gone bad. Now that Wanda is back to her old self, Connie has opened the store Monday through Saturday and lets Wanda run it durin' the week. It really is a win/win situation, if you know what I mean.

## Lot #14

As you can guess, Dottie Lamb of Lot #14 is more than thrilled at how well Lamb's Super Store is doin'. She and her daughter, Opal, of Lot #1 never imagined that the loss of their original store to that freakish fire would've turned out to be such a blessin' in disguise. And as you've read already, Dottie and Opal ain't the only ones doin' well with the new Lamb business. Why, even trailer park manager and business owner Ben Beaver, who shares Dottie's trailer, got into the game as well. I mentioned in my BBQ book that Dottie and Ben had been talkin' about openin' a section in the new Lamb's Super Store that'd be a scaled-down version of the liquor store Ben already owns. Well, sure enough, they've agreed to give it a try and business has been great. Of course it came as a shock to us on account of the fact that we live in a rural area where most folks are good old dyed-in-the-wool Baptists. We thought that people would rather park behind Ben Beaver's current liquor store and sneak in the side door like they do now when they want a bottle of hooch. Well, the business comin' in and out of that fenced-in portion towards the back of Lamb's Super Store just goes to show that we was wrong. It also goes to show that Sister Bertha was right: More Methodists *have* moved into the surroundin' area.

They tried two different names for Lamb's Super Store's liquor section. The first one was Ben and Dottie's Liquor Emporium, and they had a big picture of Ben and Dottie right there on the front. That one did all right, but when they went with a big photo of Dottie's dog-ugly daughter hangin' on the fenced-in area instead and changed the name to Opal's Liquor Barn, business went nuts. They went through more alcohol than an Episcopalian church fund-raiser. Of course my theory is that the larger-than-life photo of Opal probably scared most them folks into drinkin', or maybe people mistook it to be a kind of sideshow freak booth at first and then when they saw Opal workin' the cash register, they just bought a bottle to get a closer look. In any case, they went with Opal's Liquor Barn, which is very appropriate when you consider Opal's got the face for a barn and real strong drink. It does make one wonder why Ben would allow one of his businesses to be named after Dottie's child. But to be honest, we all knew somethin' was goin' on with Ben and Dottie ever since he moved in with her. And us folks over at the High Chaparral got an even better insight into their "friendship" just recently.

It was about three o'clock in the mornin' when me, my husband, Dew, and everybody else at the High Chaparral were awakened by these screams for help. Of course, the menfolk hurriedly threw on some clothes and ran out to see what was goin' on while we ladies threw on our house robes, touched up our makeup and hair, and then followed close behind. It was Dottie, and she was screamin' bloody murder, without a lick of makeup on and her hair up in curlers. It seemed that Ben had gotten in his wheelchair and had made a middle-of-the-night bathroom run. Well, the toilet in the master bathroom of that trailer home that Dottie and her late husband, Laverne, had bought back in 1973 finally gave way and went crashin' through the floor with Ben on it. God bless him, he was stuck under her trailer with nothin' but a pair of socks and a washcloth that Dottie had seen fit to throw down to him before runnin' off to get help. Of course the menfolk got poor embarrassed Ben out with nothin' more than his pride hurt. And the next day, Dottie and Ben went out and bought a new trailer, which was delivered later that week. I don't know if it was the fact that Ben had fallen through the master bathroom floor and not the guest bathroom, or that Ben and Dottie had bought the new trailer together, or just that the guest bed was still made up when us ladies got over to Lot #14 and started snoopin' around while Ben was bein' rescued, which led us to believe that Ben and Dottie are an actual item. I don't know, but I can tell you that if somethin' ever happens to my husband, Dew, in the middle of the night, regardless of how life-threatenin' it might be, I'm at least gonna take the time to fix my makeup and do my hair before I go runnin' out into the street. Oh well, some of us were brought up better than others.

## Lot #15

Do y'all remember how I told y'all earlier in this section of the book how my mother-in-law, Momma Ballzak, had accidentally bought the *Pangburn Bugle*? Well, she ended up sellin' it to Donny and Kenny over at Lot #15. She didn't want it, and the boys thought it would be a great way to add more goodwill and culture to our little community. Personally I think the real reason they bought the paper was so they could plug their As Time Goes By Antique Store, and their cause for the better treatment of animals. I'd say I wished 'em the best, but as anyone who's picked up a recent copy of the paper knows, they don't need it. Already they've taken what was a wonderful newspaper that my dear friends Elmer and Lovie Birch had published successfully for several years before recently movin' to Florida, and made it even better. Why, the boys gave it a facelift with a full-color front page on every issue, changed the newspaper's name, and even went so far as changin' the daily content inside. Now when we read it we are happily surprised to find a lot more columns on helpful hints, entertainment gossip, list of top dance music hits, cross stitchin' tips and patterns, decoratin' dos and don'ts, as well as color commentary on events takin' place across the state. And all the scores from the weekly canasta tournaments are posted right there at the top of the sports page. They've also added a new section that features the local garden of the week, and everyone is just waitin' with baited breath for the cannin' and picklin' section that they promise to include when spring rolls around. And naturally, as y'all might have guessed, twice a month they carry my very own personal syndicated column called "Trailer Talk." The paper seems to be doin' very well, and, accordin' to Kitty Chitwood over at the Gas and Smokes Convenience Store, the new and improved *Daily Bugle Bead* is actually sellin' better than *Grit*. I know everybody at the High Chaparral Trailer Park has the paper delivered, and yes, that includes Sister Bertha. Keep up the good work, Kenny and Donny!

## Lot #16

Unfortunately even Momma Ballzak's little part of the world, which is better known as Lot #16, has been affected by this terrible economy. Just like Ollie White of Lot #10, my husband, Dew's momma was recently laid off. We were all surprised when she was regrettably informed that startin' immediately she would no longer be needed to work behind the register at the restaurant she'd been at for almost fifty years. Sure, she was hurt, but she understood, and she quickly forgot the pain of losin' a job she'd enjoyed doin' for well over half her life once she'd knocked off half a bottle of scotch. Of course she'd done that every day around 4:30 when she'd gotten off work. Mind you, Momma Ballzak wasn't gonna starve. She still had her lucrative trailer park Tupperware business, where she'd get together with women in a hostess's home and show off her collection of old used plastic butter, margarine, sour cream, and other assorted product dishes. She'd then take orders from the gals, which she immediately filled from the stash in the back of her car trunk. The money she made off of that was enough to keep her in cigarettes and liquor for years, and her job cleanin' rooms down at the R.U. Inn covered her food costs. But she still would've liked to be able to have that extra income so she could live easily (she won't take a penny from me or my husband, Dew).

As luck would have it, within just weeks a brand-new job opportunity fell right into her lap. Actually it fell in her trailer. You see, one night when she had the then assistant town mortician Vance Pool (better known to some of y'all as exotic male dancer Vance Poole) of Lot #19 and his roommates, Harry and Leroy (also known as Poole's sidekick male dance team, the Beef Stick Boys) over for dinner and a snort of hooch, the chair that Vance was seated in gave way under the pressure. Well, he went crashin' to her trailer floor like a bag of bricks. As he picked himself up, he noticed the lovely floral arrangement of plastic flowers that Momma Ballzak had settin' on a table directly behind where he was seated. Well, long story short, he was so taken by this arrangement that he asked her if she'd be interested in joinin' him in this little endeavor down at the funeral home that he was gonna be takin' on soon (you'll have to go down to Lot #19 for all the details on that project). He wanted her to do floral arrangements usin' only the best plastic flowers that money can buy. Of course, after Momma Ballzak had made it clear that her job down at the R.U. Inn and the trailer park Tupperware business of hers had to come first, she accepted. She's always enjoyed workin' with her hands. I have a feelin' that's most likely on account of how she has to have a drink to steady 'em first.

Once me and my husband, Dew, found out about this new job of hers we called up Vance on the phone and told him that we were overjoyed he was able to use her, but we wanted to make sure that she would be able to rest every once in a while. After all, she ain't a spring chicken. He assured us that not only would she be able to take several breaks while she was on the job, but that they even had a little makeshift break room right in the funeral home where she could set back in a chair or prop her feet up on a comfortable sofa. As you can guess, that phone call relieved our worries and made us feel good about the new line of work that Momma Ballzak was takin' on. I only wish I could say the same thing about the next time we spoke with Vance on the phone just a month later, but to be honest, "feelin' good" and "worry free" were the last words I'd use to describe the incident.

It was almost five in the afternoon mountain time when the phone in our Commerce City, Colorado, holiday quad-wide trailer started ringin'. Me and my husband, Dew, had gone up to the beautiful town located just outside of Denver to try to get away from the hot summer Arkansas heat. As many of y'all know, we do this little commute on a yearly basis now, as well as when I've got to be close to a big airport like Denver International Airport so I can do my publicity travelin'. Anyways, the voice on the other end turned out to be Vance. It seemed that Momma Ballzak had taken a break and decided to lie down on the sofa in the break room. Well, she'd already started to hit the bottle, which Vance allowed since it didn't affect her floral arrangin', and I guess that along with the fact that she hadn't slept well the night before basically knocked her out like a light. As she lay fast asleep, a team of morticians who'd driven up from Dallas to pick up a body that Vance had on ice of a person that died in their sleep while on vacation over in Searcy showed up to get the body. Vance went on to say that since he was so busy with a funeral that was takin' place already, he just told the fellas to go in the back and get it themselves. Well, as you've most likely guessed, the Dallas morticians took off back to Texas with Momma Ballzak in the back of the hearse. Accordin' to Vance, they was around twenty miles outside of Texarkana when Momma Ballzak came to and started screamin' bloody murder, which in turn scared the heck out the poor fellas, causin' 'em to fishtail that hearse around and right off into a ditch. Both the men suffered minor injuries, but the coffin Momma Ballzak was in came flyin' out of that spinnin' car and landed in a nearby river. Well, somehow she and that death box were finally fished in to shore somewhere around Shreveport minutes before Vance called us. He said she was sober, but fine. Of course that worried the heck out my husband, Dew, so me and him caught the first flight out to Shreveport. We told the police to just get her a nice room at a hotel and we'd take care of the bill when we got there. If I hadn't been so panicked and in a rush, I've have thought to tell them to make sure there was no minibar in that hotel room. Who'd have thought an old tiny woman like that could go through one of them in three hours. Anyways, we got her back home and she's doin' just great. She loves workin' as a plastic floral arranger and Vance made her a little sign for her to wear from now on when she goes into the break room that reads DO NOT REMOVE FROM THE FUNERAL HOME.

## Lot #17

Faye Faye LaRue of Lot #17 has really discovered her true gift in life. She can tell you all about the future, but y'all already know that because I told you so in my last book. But since then, this full-time stripper, owner of the Danglin' Tassel, and archrival of my sister, Donna Sue, has made even more predictions. Why, she told them midget cliff divers down at the Taco Tackle Shack North to watch their backs, and you already know what's goin' on with them (see Lot #3). She let Anita Biggon of Lot #2 know that there would be a mysterious stranger in her life, and I'll be doggone if she didn't get a call that very same night from a man who wanted her to sign up for a new long-distance carrier. When she told him to never call her again and then asked the fella's name, he hung up. That Faye Faye LaRue was right on the money with that one. And she recently told me that I'd soon see things in a new light and it wasn't more than a month that my kitchen light went out and I had to replace it. God bless her, she's got the gift, and she has agreed to do that trailer park horoscope book. Oh, just y'all wait till you get to see her predictions about your life come true. It really is fun. Of course, seein' how busy she is at the Danglin' Tassel as well as with all her psychic readin' sessions that she's been doin' since we last talked, it may be years before she gets that book done. You know, I ought to have her give me a prediction about that as well.

Faye Faye's daughter, Tina Faye Stopenblotter, is doin' real good with that motel she opened up in honor of her late daddy and former state senator and senior's rights crusader R. U. Watts. And business ain't the only thing that's hoppin' down at the R.U. Inn. Durin' the end of the week Tina Faye also has added a big band that plays swing music from 5:00 P.M. to 7:00 P.M. Friday and Saturday nights in the ballroom. It seems her "sixty-niner special," where folks sixty or over can check into any of the twelve vacant rooms for only $9.00 a night has really drawn in the older crowd (It used to be thirteen rooms, but two of the employees over at the Blue Whale Strip Club have rented out one of the rooms indefinitely). Anyways, on account of that big band music she has goin', Tina Faye is seein' folks come from all corners of the state to dance to the sounds that made Glenn Miller and Count Basie famous. The only problem is you got lots of folks around these parts that attend churches that shun public dancin'. So what Tina Faye has done is to dim the lights and fill up the room with fog from one of them machines. This way folks can jitterbug until the cows come home, or at least until 7:00 P.M., without havin' to worry about who sees 'em. And, boy, you should hear the good time these folks have as they relive their youths dancin' like they did back in 1940. Of course I'm sure that when they cut a rug back then you didn't have all those sounds of knees crackin' and backs poppin' like you hear now when the joint starts jumpin'.

Tina Faye says she's also had some real freaky folks pull into the front of the motel and ask some real bizarre questions that she's able to handle without bein' shocked, on account of her mother's line of work. I don't know what makes people do weird stuff like that, but when she's told me what these folks have asked, well, to be honest, I even blushed. I guess some people are just plain old stupid. In any case, if you're ever up our way and you happen to need a place to lay your head, just look for the big sign out by the highway that reads HOME OF THE SIXTY-NINER, R.U. INN, SWINGERS WELCOMED.

## Lot #18

Y'all already know what's goin' on in me and my husband, Dew's lives, but for those of y'all who don't, well, just go to my Web page at www.rubyannboxcar.com to find out.

## Lot #19

Now it's official: Vance Poole, the American Tenderloin, and his Beef Stick Boys have gone into semiretirement. Sure, they'll still do the occasional birthday or, even as was the case with Lulu Bell and Billy Bob, a bachelorette and bachelor party from time to time, but for the most part, they've packed away their thongs. This means that Vance Pool, as you know he adds the "e" on the end of his name when he's dancin', will be able to follow his dream. For a while now he'd been the assistant mortician at the local funeral home. He loved his job, but he really wanted more. Well, with the announcement this past September that Arleen Sprig would be puttin' the funeral home up for sale so she could retire with her brother to Clearwater, Kansas, it looked like Vance would finally see his dream come true. He took out a loan from one of them online lenders and purchased the place lock, stock, and barrel. I tell you, Vance was like a kid in a candy store. He even took out a full-page ad in the *Daily Bugle Bead* announcin' that the Vance Pool Funeral Center would be unlike any funeral home in the U.S. He said that this had been a passion of his, and he wanted to put a new face on the world of death, so just as soon as they'd finished the remodlin' of the old buildin', he'd share more information with us. Personally, I thought he should follow that dream just as long as it meant he kept his dang clothes on. Well, what would happen in the week to follow threw all of us for a loop. This new style of funeral home service that Vance had promised us turned out to actually be somethin' that really could revolutionize the funeral business as we knew it. What he did was, well, let me just explain how it works.

Let's just say that my Me-Ma were to pass away and we had her hauled down to Vance's place. When it came time for the viewin', you'd load up the car and drive down to the funeral center, where you'd find signs that'd direct you to a car lane that'd guide you up to a window, kind of like they got at the drive-thru over at Anita's Bar and Grill. There you'd be greeted by Vance, who'd reach out that window and offer you a book for you to sign so you and your grievin' family can keep a record of who attended, just like at a regular funeral. Then he'd hand y'all some funeral leaflets as well a tape player with a cassette already in it. Vance would finally thank you for comin' and ask you to please pull up to the next window where you'd be received by my mother-in-law, Momma Ballzak.

At this window you could place and pay for your flower order to show your respects for my Me-Ma. And the good thing is that the arrangements run anywhere from $10, which is a plastic tulip in a vase with the word "Bye" displayed on it, all the way up to $150, which gets you five dozen plastic lilies in a beautiful vase with the words "Dear Friend, we'll keep you in our hearts and minds until we see you again on those streets of gold," emblazoned on a gold-leaf plaque. After you'd ordered your flowers, Momma Ballzak would instruct you to pull up to the next window where you could place a food order with Harry. You could get a bag of popcorn, hot dogs, ice cream, soda pops, or coffee, or even chili when in season. Once you'd gotten your food item, Harry would tell you to drive on.

As you pulled away from that window you'd see a sign that'd instruct you to press the play button on the tape player. As you waited in line in the comfort of your car, you'd hear a brief bio on my Me-Ma as well as a few comments from me and the rest of her loved ones.

As the line continued to move you'd finally come to one of those tollgatelike arms that prevent your car from movin' forward. At this point in the line you'd be instructed by a sign to put your car in park. Once you'd done that you'd notice that you was right next to a big glass window with large velvet burgundy curtains. There'd be a change basket in front of the window as well as a sign that read 50¢ FOR 30 SECONDS. When you tossed in your change, the velvet curtains would pull open to reveal Me-Ma peacefully restin' in her casket, which had carefully been propped up to an eighty-degree angle for better viewin'. A light from directly in front of your car would then quickly flash. All along the floor by Me-Ma's casket would be the flower arrangements that viewers like yourself had purchased. Next to each arrangement would be a great big sign with bold letters statin' who the flowers were from. And of course yours would be right up front for everyone to see. Also out in front of the window would be an ATM-lookin' machine where you could enter your credit card, debit card, or bank card and order a quick floral upgrade, which would mean that your arrangement would be immediately pulled from the window display before anyone else would be able to see it, upgraded to a larger version, and then put back into the window, all for a small fee of course. Once your time ran out, the curtains would quickly swing closed, and the arm would raise, allowin' you to pull forward.

The last window you'd come across would be the memorial shop, where Elroy would help you with your purchases of buttons, notebooks, coffee mugs, and T-shirts all bearin' a photo of Me-Ma as well as the date she was born and the date she passed. But that's not all. In order to help you to remember your visit, you could also purchase an 8" x 10" photo of you and the deceased that was snapped when the velvet curtains opened durin' your viewin' time. There would be several lovely frames to choose from, too. Once you'd made your selections and returned the cassette player and tape to Elroy, he'd push a button, which'd cause the large metal spikes in the road just in front of your car to go down in the ground so you could exit safely.

Well, as you can easily guess, this funeral thing of Vance's caught on like wildfire with people comin' from all over the state to have their loved ones viewin'. I don't know if it was 'cause of the new way the whole thing was handled or the fact that the immediate family got a cut of the sales from the viewin', but everyone wanted to get in on it. Accordin' to Vance, the Funeral Center has been doin' so well, he's thinkin' about expandin' to Fort Smith and all the way over to Springfield, Missouri.

## Lot #20

Our newest member to the High Chaparral Trailer Park is a gal that many of y'all have heard me mention before. And if you've read my sister's book, *Donna Sue's Down Home Trailer Park Bartending Guide,* then you already know all about her. She's a fellow dancer down at the Blue Whale Strip Club with my sister, Donna Sue, and a gal that is always glad to see you. Yes, I'm talkin' about the one and only Little Linda. Now, I know that some of y'all are already askin' how was we able to sneak the wildest gal in Arkansas into the High Chaparral without upsettin' folks on the residents' board like Sister Bertha? Well that's easy. Sister Bertha's got feet like a truck driver. I'm here to tell you that the gal has got more corns on her feet than Iowa's got in its fields. And the poor thing has calluses the size of baseballs. Anyways, Little Linda owns the Beauty Barge, the state's only floatin' full-service beauty parlor, where both Nellie Tinkle, who happens to be on the residents' board, and Dottie Lamb, who happens to share a trailer with residents' board member Ben Beaver, get their hair done. Well, Little Linda's got this gal down there that can work wonders on feet. And even though Sister Bertha might despise Little Linda and her partyin' ways, she can't turn down a six months' supply of foot rubs.

Now I got to add here that the thing parked in Lot #20 ain't your common trailer. You see, right now all Little Linda has is an old beat-up RV that one of her admirers gave her before he went off to serve his life-in-prison sentence. And Lord bless her, it also happens to be the only vehicle that the poor gal has that runs right now. So when she needs to go somewhere she has to unhook the sewer and water line, and then she can head out, leavin' the lot vacant. But till she gets that broken-down Pacer of hers fixed, that RV is all that runs. And I say that loosely on account of the fact that she moved into the park in September and she's already had to have it jumped more times than I can count. Luckily she's got a good rapport with the boys over in Lot #19 as well as Anita across the way in Lot #2 or she'd be stuck there with a pair of jumper cables in her hands. But even after she gets it goin', there ain't no guarantee it's gonna go anywhere. That poor thing has went from Lot #20 to bein' Lot #19½ on more than four occasions. Of course she has a really nice 2001 trailer home that she plans on movin' into just as soon as the state police can track it down and evict them folks right out of there that the bank turned around and foreclosed on. In the meantime, regardless if you see anything parked in the space or not, don't try to park there, cause Lot #20 belongs to Little Linda. Welcome aboard, gal!

# Chapter 1

# Around the Trailer

*Unbeknownst to Faye Faye LaRue of Lot #17, a swarm of accidentally soaked hornets were makin' their way to express their thoughts on her annual hosin' down of her trailer. Because of the high amounts of toxins already in Faye Faye's body on account of her many years of heavy drinkin', the massive hornet stings acted more like an all over treatment of botox, given' her the body of a twenty-one-year-old. Even after promises of large monetary gifts, me and the rest of the High Chaparral Trailer Park board had to later reject her dire request to operate a beehive on her trailer lot.*

The big thing right now on the TVs in the trailer parks across the English-speakin' world is them shows where neighbors switch houses with each other and they redo a room in the other one's abode. I tell you, we get such a kick out of them shows. Not only do they use colors and materials that none of us have ever thought of tryin' (who'd have ever come up with the notion of gluin' hay to your wall rather than usin' wallpaper), but they all seem to have a good time doin' the projects. Of course some of 'em tend to get upset when they later find that the room in their home ain't like they'd thought or wished it'd turn out to be. At this point in the program I just yell at 'em via the TV screen, "Hello, don't you folks watch these shows before you sign up to be on 'em?" Needless to say, I add 'em to my prayer list, askin' that the good Lord will see fit to give 'em brains or at least some kind of thought process before they jump into things. I use the same prayer for them that I use for the fellas that come home with my sister late in the middle of the night.

Let's be honest with each other for a moment and say that there really ain't a lot you can do to a trailer home's interior unless you happen to be one of them folks over on that Web page www.tradingtrailers.com. If you ain't never been there, you really have to check it out. They pull off some real nice trailer fixin'-uppin'. Of course the difference between them and the other shows with nonwheeled homes is that trailer people are always happy with the way that their rooms was redesigned on account of the fact that they didn't have to do it themselves, if you know what I mean. And even though I'm gifted when it comes to good taste,

I'm leavin' all the trailer room designin' to these experts. Oh, and I've also added 'em to my prayer list. I'm askin' the good Lord to send 'em to my sister's trailer 'cause, God bless her, that old cow can use all the help she can get. Of course if they do ever make it over to her trailer home they won't be able to use anythin' that heats up like a solderin' iron or a hot glue gun on account of all the thick liquor fumes that fill Donna Sue's single-wide over on Lot #6. It's gonna take 'em longer than two days to air it out as well.

What we're gonna do in this chapter is talk about the exterior or outside of your trailer. Now you certainly can paint your trailer a new color, after all, I'm sure y'all recall in my first book, *Ruby Ann's Down Home Trailer Park Cookbook,* how the Janssen twins mean-spiritedly spray-painted their folks' mobile home Smurf blue. So that can be done. I don't advise it on account of it lookin' real tacky as the paint gets old. And you sure can't just scrap it off without tearin' up the outside of your trailer home. But don't fret, 'cause I'm gonna tell you how we give our trailers a new fresh look every year up here at the High Chaparral Trailer Park. So put on some clothes and grab the duct tape, 'cause it's time to make your home look beautiful.

Every year here at the High Chaparral right around May or June, Ben Beaver makes us all give our trailer homes a good washin' down. I should stop here and clarify that when I say every year, I mean startin' this year. You see, back when his wife, Dora, was alive, he never made us do no kind of trailer cleanin'. All we did was just let Mother Nature and God take care of all that. The rain would come, do what it'd do to rinse off the aluminum walls, then the snow would fall and finally melt the dirt away. That was good enough back then. But after Dora Beaver accidentally pulled that rack of vodka bottles down on herself at Beaver Liquors and Wines while she was cleanin', things changed. You'd have thought that Ben would've learned his lesson that no good can come from cleanin' after that, but oh no. Once Dottie Lamb came into the picture cleanliness became next to godliness, even though I don't know how godly his move from Lot #7 over to Dottie Lamb's trailer a few months after the passin' of his wife was, but I'm not one to gossip or judge people. I'll just leave that in the capable hands of Sister Bertha. In any case, now we all got to get out there and clean our trailers between May and June or Ben will hire someone to come out and do it for us. He then will add a charge of $60 on to your next month's rent regardless of the size of your trailer home. Some folks at the High Chaparral think he started this on account of tryin' to make the trailer park look good in order to impress Dottie. Personally I think it all came about on account of the abundance of high-pressure water sprayers that Dottie had down at Lamb's Super Store. I told her not to order those since nobody will wash their car or truck at home when the new Billy Bob's Suck and Squirt Car Wash only charges 5¢ a minute to use, and it's got the latest in state-of-the-art high-tech vacuums and high-pressure sprayin' wands. But of course she didn't listen and now she's got a whole section in the yard and gardenin' department with nothin' but high-pressure sprayers. In any case, I can tell y'all that not one of us at the High Chaparral bought one of them sprayers just out of spite, on account of this new trailer washin' thing. Instead we just came up with our own special way of cleanin' the outsides of our trailers, which I'm gonna share with y'all here in just a minute. But first there are a few prewashin' things that we need to go over.

The last thing you want to do is to get water in your trailer when you're washin' her down. Nobody wants a soaked couch, wet bed, or a drenched shag carpet for that matter. So you'll need to start off checkin' your windows for cracks. If you got a big crack like some folks in the trailer park have, you're gonna want to take care of that right off the bat. Grab some duct tape and cut off a strip that's just long enough to lay over the crack in the window as shown in the photo next door.

Make sure you press down tightly so the tape ain't got no air between it and the window. Just don't push too hard or you're most likely gonna end up goin' through the screen. Personally, I suggest that you put a strip of duct tape along the crack on just the inside. After all, there ain't no reason to have to take that dang window screen off if you ain't got to.

Now, if your crack is bigger than normal, like my sister Donna Sue's got, then you're gonna need more than just duct tape. Go ahead and put the duct tape on as we talked about, but then take an old plastic trash bag and cut out a square that's just big enough to cover the crack. Duct-tape that over the crack like I show you in the picture.

Next, take a piece of cardboard and cut out a square that's just a bit bigger than the plastic one that you done got on the window. Duct-tape that over the plastic square. That should keep your trailer dry.

If you're missin' a window all together on account of either a robbery or 'cause you locked your keys inside your trailer, well then, you're gonna need to patch that up inside and out with some big pieces of cardboard, plastic, and duct tape first before you take the hose to your trailer home. I ain't no Mr. Bob Vila, so you're on your own on this one, hon. Sorry.

Once your cracks have been filled, you're gonna want to give your window the old candle test. Take a candle that you've lighted and slowly pass it along the window frame. If it goes out or flickers a lot in one area, then you got an air leak in that section. If that's the case, you're gonna have to take a big plastic bag and some duct tape, and tape that plastic over your window so the water don't get in. Make sure you do this on every window after you've taped over your cracks. When I do this, I make sure to use a candle with a nice fragrance to it so I not only prepare my home for a good washin', but I also spread a pleasant aroma throughout.

Just know that you're gonna have to tape up some plastic around your doors or place some big towels around the door frame. An example of this is illustrated in this drawin' here. Once you've done this, you're ready to move on.

If you've had problems with a leaky roof, this is the best time to go ahead and fix it. I am by no means recommendin' that you get a professional tar or roof repair person to come out. Why spend that much money when you can do it yourself? Just go out and get yourself some of that waterproof caulkin' like you use when you install sinks or tubs and give those tears, rips, or holes a good hefty squirt. If upon appraisal of your roof you see that it's mostly just holes and you can't afford to go out and get the caulkin', then just plug 'em up with some freshly chewed bubble gum. Then give that area on the roof three or four good coats of leftover latex paint that you got stored in your closet or some that you borrow from a neighbor. That should hold up for a while. And so what if you don't get the whole thing fixed. After all, the sound of runnin' water is very calmin' and soothin' to most folks. Just pretend that the sounds the drippin' water makes when it hits that cookin' pot you got on the floor to catch the leak is just like one of them fancy high-dollar relaxation fountains. Why, I know Momma Ballzak even puts gravel in the bottom of her leak-catchin' pots to create that exact effect when the TV and radio forecast rain. Just make sure that you got your rain lamp out of the way of the leak. Regardless of the lamp's name, real water and that mineral oil that runs down them strands don't mix. So just move it.

OK, we're finally ready for our trailer washin'. You're gonna need a workin' water spout, a long hose, a broom, a piece of rope or string about three feet long, an old towel, and one regular bottle of dish-washin' soap. That's it. Well, that and an hour or two of your time. Before you actually turn on the water, you'll need to hook up the hose, take the old towel and wrap it around the bristle part of the broom, and finally secure it to the broom with that rope or string.

Next you'll take your bottle of dish-washin' soap and with the bottle held as high as you can raise it, tilt the opened end downward towards the trailer. As the liquid starts to come out, walk from one end of the trailer wall that you are cleanin' to the other end. You might have to give the bottle a little squeeze as you walk to make sure you've got a steady stream flowin' all the way across the side of the trailer. Now turn on the water.

Startin' at the bottom of the trailer, work your stream of water up until you get to the soap, which by now should be slightly runnin' down the trailer. When your water hits that dish-washin' liquid it will start to create a little lather. Just continue to work that lather up towards the top of the trailer. If some of it wants to run down, that's fine. Once you've done this about two or three yards, go back and start shootin' that water towards the top of the trailer. Now work it from the top all the way down. This should help to rinse away all the soap lather that you had worked to the top. When you've rinsed off the suds and have gotten to the point where you stopped washin', begin the whole process over again. Just make sure that you give all them exterior Christmas lights that hang out on the trailer all year long a good blast of water.

And do your best to avoid hornets' or wasps' nests. If you get to one while you clean, stay away from it or simply take it down with some of that professional hornet spray. Whatever you do, don't pull an Ollie White and go after the darn thing with a can of hair spray and a lighter for cryin' out loud. Sure she burnt down the nest with that homemade flamethrower, but she caught her trailer on fire again in the process. Hubert had to hook it up to his truck and yet again race it down to the boat docks and back it into the lake. You'd have thought Ollie would have learned her lesson the first time when she set her cardboard fireplace ablazin'. I told y'all about that story in my BBQ cookbook. Needless to say, this year alone that trailer has seen the lake four and a half times (on one occasion, halfway home they realized the fire wasn't totally out and had to do a partial redunkin').

If you notice that you got a few places that need a little more help gettin' washed, take that makeshift scrubbin' stick that you conjured up with the broom, towel, and rope, and get goin' on that area. Just wet the spot down and apply a little soap to the scrubbin' stick. But be careful not to put too much pressure on any certain area or you're likely to wipe off some paint. The good Lord knows you don't want some freaky-lookin' trailer with a bald spot on it. So rub gently.

When you've finished one side, grab your tools and move on to the next side. Just continue this process until you've done all four sides. By the way, if you got a two-story trailer like mine, you might want to go onto your roof and squirt the dish-washin' soap along the very top of the trailer just to make sure you got it all covered. But if you ain't no kind of a star, then of course you won't have to worry about that at all.

I got to be honest and tell y'all that the trailers do look a lot nicer after they've had a good washin'. And it also makes the outside Christmas lights shine so much brighter with all that dirt, dust, and crud cleaned off of 'em. So maybe this once-a-year trailer cleanin' ain't all that bad after all. Actually it might be somethin' that y'all might want to try and start in the trailer park where you live.

Oh, there is one thing I did forget to mention, and that is simply that if you got to pay for your water usage in your lot, to heck with everything I told you to do in this chapter. Just pay that dang $60.

## Ask Ruby Ann . . .

Dear Ruby Ann,

My husband and I have decided it's time to replace the living room furniture, so we are giving it to our daughter and shopping for new items. We both fell in love with a beautiful wicker couch and love seat, but before we buy it we wanted to get your opinion on using wicker in the living room.

Whitney B.
Pueblo, CO

Dear Whitney,

Yes, I understand how important it is to swap out your furniture from time to time, and the fact that your daughter will be gettin' it makes it even nicer. I say go ahead and get that wicker set if you love it. After all, it is your home, ain't it? Of course, you won't be able to have company over or if you do you'll have to set 'em in somethin' else. I mean how embarrassin' is it gonna be for you and your husband when y'all got to yell out, "Stop," to a larger guest as he starts to set down on your wicker? I'd love to be a fly on the wall when you try to explain to him why you almost went into cardiac arrest. I know you won't see my big behind over at your home, regardless of what kind of food you're servin'. There ain't nothin' more unnervin' for large folks than the sight of wicker furniture, unless of course it's flimsy foldin' chairs. And I know that if I end up on the floor 'cause you weren't thoughtful enough to buy furniture that could support my doggone weight, I'd be slappin' your wicker-lovin' behinds with a lawsuit so fast your heads would spin. But hey, you and your husband go right ahead and buy whatever y'all want.

Love, Kisses, and Trailer Park Wishes,
Ruby Ann Boxcar

# Chapter 2

# Thirty-Some-Odd Years of Beauty Secrets

*With the help of her husband, Dick, dear Opal Lamb-Inman of Lot #1 helps to demonstrate the magic of cosmetics by havin' makeup applied to just one side of her face. Dick Inman says he's always enjoyed applyin' makeup and adds that the secret to puttin' Opal's cosmetics on is to do it in the mornin' before Dick puts his contact in.*

Are you tired of goin' to work everyday and seein' that hot sexy man without him seein' you? How many times have you pumped your own gas at that station only to be overlooked by that attractive clerk that you'd love to go out with? Can you possibly attend one more party and end up settin' all alone in some corner while all the good-lookin' men chat up the other girls? Or are you married gals startin' to feel like your husbands would rather watch one of those horrid feminine product commercials than look at you? Well, don't worry, help is finally here! Of course you must understand that it would take a whole book for me to share all the tips that you need, but I'll still be able to give you enough trailer park makeup pointers in the limited space that I've got to get you gals on the right track. All you got to do is believe in yourselves and follow my directions to the letter if you want to see things change in your world.

Seein' how I am limited in space, I'm gonna choose the part of the face that I personally think y'all need the most help with at this time. Mind you, there are some of you ladies out there that could use a whole makeover, so this will only be like a drop in the bucket for you, but try it anyways. With that said, let me finally reveal the area that we're gonna work on this go around. And that part is simply the eye. That's right, ladies, I'm gonna show you how to pick out the best color of eye shadow so that you ain't never got to worry about if this shade is good or not for you. I'm kind of like them scrubbin' bubbles on account of the fact that I've already done all of the hard work so you don't have to-o-o-o-o-o-o-o.

As you can probably guess, not a day goes by that someone on the street, in a store, or even on a plane don't come up to me and ask me who in heck does my makeup. The reason for this is simple. They can tell that I care about the way that I look. They can see that regardless of how bad my life might be, I still find the time to make myself into a thing of beauty. And now, ladies, with my help you can be on your way to bein' objects of desire. It's pretty easy and won't cost you much. With that in mind, grab that cosmetic bag and let's get started.

When I told a few of my friends who happened to be holdin' a spontaneous gatherin' outside the Piggly Wiggly in the neighborin' town of Searcy that I was goin' to write a chapter in this book on eye makeup, they almost swallowed their Skoal spit. "Ruby Ann," they said, "why would you want to devote a whole chapter to eyes?"

So many women don't understand how important proper eye makeup really is. They just don't get it. Without our eyes, we might as well be blind. But the good news is that beautifyin' our eyes is easier than my sister at last call! Just follow my professional instructions and we'll have you on the road to lookin' as good as any of the gals at the High Chaparral Trailer Park, or the Blue Whale Strip Club for that matter.

The first thing we need to do is take a look at the eye shadows that you already got in your collection of cosmetics. If you are like most poor gals who didn't get to go to beauty school like I did, then you probably got a whole bunch of different shades of eye shadow. You most likely even got colors that you wear durin' the day and some that you wear at night. Why, I bet you've even got your shades that you wear for special events as well. But that's all right, and nothin' to be ashamed of. After all, you didn't know any better, and that's why I'm here to help. So let's get started by examinin' each shadow.

## Browns, Grays, and Earth Tones

Brown colors as well as grays and earth tones are all wrong on the eye. Now, there are many that'll yell, holler, and just downright spit on me for sayin' this, and that's fine, 'cause we're Americans and we can say and believe whatever we want to, regardless of how wrong it might be! And I know that one day they'll come to their senses and admit that I'm right about this. But anyways, the reason that I don't like 'em is simply 'cause they create a look that some have labeled "natural." When applied correctly, they make you look like you ain't wearin' a lick of makeup, and when applied incorrectly, they make you look like some kind of freaky gigantic rabid mutant raccoon. I think it's fair to say none of us want to look like a raccoon, nor do any of us want to look like we're not wearin' makeup. As I've always understood it, the reason we put on makeup in the first place is to get as far away from that natural look that we already have. After all, is there one of you self-respectin' gals that'll leave the house without first consultin' with your cosmetic bag? Why, a twister could be knockin' on your door, and before you'd leave in search of some kind of shelter, you'd be in your bathroom puttin' a little bit of lipstick and blush on! Am I right? You're doggone right I am! Ladies, in all honesty, we just don't want to look natural, we want to look beautiful. Just remember, and I mean this as nice as possible, Amish women look natural, but Ms. Raquel Welch looks beautiful. So unless you like bein' mistaken for a giant member of the Procyonidae family or plan on ridin' around in a buggy, pull all of those browns, beiges, and grays out of your makeup collection and set 'em aside in a box for the kids to use on Halloween.

## Greens

Every woman, regardless if she lives in a mansion or under a bridge, has a green eye shadow in her cosmetic reserves. Even I've got green eye shadow in my private hoard, but there are only three times a year you'll catch it on my eyes: St. Patrick's Day, Halloween, and durin' the Christmas season. That's it! And the reason I don't wear it any of the other days of the year is 'cause of the male gender. That's right! Oh, I'll be the first to say that green is a very pretty color, but in a man's eyes, it's more then just a color, it's a big old reminder sign. Have you ever seen somethin' that reminded you of somethin' else? Maybe you were workin' in the kitchen and caught the sight of a mustard bottle for just a split second. Before you know it, that mustard bottle got you to thinkin' about a favorite yellow dress of yours that you used to wear? Do you know what I'm talkin' about? Well, this is the same kind of effect that we'll get from a man when he sees our green eye shadow. A woman, when she thinks of green, will make that connection with beautiful things like Christmas, flowers, a lovely sweet-smellin' meadow filled with fresh spring grass, or brilliant emeralds. Well, that ain't quite true when a man thinks of green. You see, ladies, it reminds him of frogs, swamps, alligators, slime, dirty gym sneakers, athlete's foot fungus, and snakes, which are about as big of a turn-on as Me-Ma in a thong! The truth of the matter is that the green will make him want to go off and find one of his male friends to talk about frogs, alligators, and snakes, or just go out and be athletic. I know that's not the effect I want my makeup to have on a man. On St. Patrick's Day, Halloween, and around Christmas, you can safely apply green to your eyes, 'cause men will associate it with the holidays, which will cancel out their normal green memories. So, ladies, you can either take the chance and use this color wisely on them holidays, or not risk it and just throw it in that box.

## Purple

Purple is one of my favorite colors. It's so vivid, fresh, and majestic, but you'll never find it on my face. Oh, I know some of you women think that purple on your eyes makes you look like lovely fresh lilacs, but trust me, in reality, it doesn't and you don't. It's so easy to apply purple eye shadow incorrectly, and the consequences can be absolutely terrible not only for you, but also for your friends and loved ones. There was a woman who used to live at the High Chaparral many years back that we all worried about for months. Her name was Billie Faye McNutt, and she and her husband kept to themselves for the most part. Well, one day out of the blue she came out of her trailer lookin' like someone had taken a baseball bat to her face. She was so bruised. Finally, after weeks of tryin' in vain to hint at how it would be all right for her to tell us what was happenin' at home, we gals took matters into our own hands! It wasn't until the ambulance had left the High Chaparral to quickly rush her husband, Mortimer's broken body to the hospital, that we ladies learnt that the supposed bruises were nothin' more than a makeup mistake. Well, needless to say, all of us gals were so embarrassed that we had whipped her husband's butt so badly over a simple case of incorrect makeup application, that we helped by doin' some of his chores till he could get back on his feet. All of this 'cause she thought the purple on her eyes made her look as beautiful as a flower. For goodness sake, ladies, and for the safety of the ones you love, put those pretty purple shadows with the rest of those discarded colors.

## Reds and Pinks

When it comes to reds and pinks, I just have two words to say, "circus clown." Unless you can shape a balloon into an animal or drive a tiny car, I'd go ahead and put them colors away as well. After all, it's that complicated.

## Yellows and Oranges

Yellows and oranges are very nice and complimentary to the skin tone for women of color, but if you've got light or medium skin, don't use 'em. If you do use these shades, then don't be offended when some man that has been flirtin' with you later pulls $50 out of his wallet and places it in your blouse. Hey, if I wear a red outfit in a cattle pasture, then I've got no reason to cuss out the bull for knockin' me on my bottom! Enough said. Into the box.

So, what color is left for us to put on our eyes? The color of the gods, Ms. Elizabeth Taylor, and most 99¢ stores, too.

## Blue

Yes, I said blue. This is a shade that's always been connected to cool, calm, fresh, and bright feelin's by both men and women. Your face will glow like the neon lights on the Las Vegas strip with blue eye shadow on your peepers. Trust me, I know, 'cause mine always does when I happen to be in Sin City. Now, I know that a lot of y'all are afraid of usin' the color blue, but let me assure you that you've got nothin' to be afraid of. As a matter of fact, many famous people, such as Cleopatra, Miss Joan Crawford, Miss Kitty from *Gunsmoke,* Miss Jane Fonda, Miss Brigitte Bardot, Mr. J. Edgar Hoover, and, of course, Miss Elizabeth Taylor have all used blue eye shadow to bring out their inner beauty. Still, I am sure that some of y'all still got doubts, so I am goin' to try and answer a few of the most commonly asked questions about this brilliant color.

**Q.** ***Won't blue eye shadow make me look cheap and easy?***
**A.** Why no! Scientists have proven that the color blue is a nonpassionate color, and I've been wearin' it for almost forty years without one inappropriate proposal. For that matter, on account of my blue eyeshadow I had to get my husband a bit tipsy before he was able to ask me to marry him.

**Q.** ***If it's a nonpassionate color, then how will I be able to draw men's attention?***

**A.** By nonpassionate, I mean that it'll not turn men on like yellow or orange will. What it'll do is draw a man's attention to you, just as anythin' of beauty will, and then, as far as the passion goes, that's up to you.

**Q.** ***Is it possible to put on too much blue?***

**A.** Blue eye shadow, unlike natural tones and purple, is one of those things that you can never overuse. The more the better as I always say!

**Q.** ***Is it possible to put on too little?***

**A.** It's definitely possible to put on too little when it comes to blue eye shadow. 'Cause of this, I've come up with a way you can test to see if you're wearin' enough. This test is so simple even Anna Nicole Smith could do it, with one breast tied behind her back. All that you do is apply what you think is the correct amount of blue to your eyes, and then shut the lights off. Wait about ten seconds and then flip the lights back on. Now, quickly look in the mirror. If the first thing that hits you is the blue on your eyes, then you've got enough on. If your lips or blush are the first things you notice, then you need to apply more blue. After that, take the test again.

**Q.** ***If blue is such a good eye color, why don't we see more women on TV or in the movies wearin' it?***

**A.** Unfortunately, modern technology has not caught up with the world of fashion. The blue messes with the TV cameras, causin' the picture on the TV to look harsh. The reason you don't find it on movie stars is 'cause of the new kinds of special effects they use in the movies, and even on TV. One of these effects is performed with a blue screen, which the actor stands in front of. Later, they add a background to the footage that appears behind the actor or wherever the blue screen was at. Anything that's blue, like blue eye shadow, will show the new background footage on it. Basically, if the actress that's wearin' blue on her eyes is filmed in front of a blue screen, and then footage of a train comin' is added to the film, you can see part of that oncomin' train on her eyes. This of course spoils the effect. In the old days, they'd just paint in the background, and that's why you saw so many actresses wearin' the popular blue eye shadow. Hopefully, some day in our near future, women in film and on the boob tube will once again be able to proudly wear this complimentary shade. I know I wear it whenever I do

TV spots, as does that gal on that one show. You know that beautiful classy gal. What's the name of that show she is on? Oh, yes, *Drew Carey*. That gal.

**Q.** ***Seein' how there are many shades of blue, which one do you recommend?***

**A.** Personally, I like to use an electric blue, but any medium to light shade will work just as nicely. Turquoise is another of my standby favorites. Stay away from the dark blues, though, 'cause they've got a tendency to blend in with your black-colored eye products like eyeliner or mascara. This, just like the browns and earth tones, creates the much dreaded Rocky the Raccoon look which you want to avoid unless you're tryin' to pick up Ranger Rick, or you're preparin' to rob a bank.

Well, I hope I've managed to answer all the questions that you might have had. When it comes to blue eye shadow, just remember what the late great hero of our country President Franklin Delano Roosevelt once said, "The only thing we've got to fear is fear itself . . . and my wife's teeth." He was right on both counts. So, what are you waitin' for? If you don't have any blue shadow, go out and get it. And then, take that eye shadow and brush, and turn yourself into that walkin' vision of pure unnatural beauty that I know you can be.

## Ask Ruby Ann . . .

Dear Ruby Ann,

I work in a theme park as one of the popular characters that you see in the parades and signin' autographs. As you can probably guess, I just love my job. My only problem is that because of the heat under those large heads I have to wear, I tend to sweat all my makeup off, so I just don't wear cosmetics at all to work. Normally that is just fine, but this new guy who is really good-lookin' has just started workin' there, and I would love to go out with him. I don't want you to think I'm ugly, but I do look much better and even feel better with makeup on. So what should I do? How can I wear my head without sweating my makeup off. Thanks for your help, Ruby Ann!

Dixie S.
Orlando, FL

Dear Dixie,

First off, let me just tell you that I love all them parks in Orlando and would love to come and see you personally if you'd just send me and my husband some passes to get into where you work for a few days. Of course a couple of free nights' stay at one of them fun hotels would be a welcome gift as well. But anyways, on to your question.

Hon, I got the perfect answer for you! All you got to do is get up about twenty minutes earlier than you normally did when you put your makeup on in the past. Go ahead and get yourself ready, and apply your cosmetics. When you've finished, go into the kitchen and put some of that paraffin wax in a skillet and turn it on to the high settin' so that it will melt. Next, open your freezer door and stick your face in the freezer. Regardless of how cold it might get or stiff your face might feel, keep it in there for at least ten minutes. When you can slap your face and not feel anything, then you know you're ready. Once you've reached this level of cold, quickly dab your whole face with the melted wax so that it's completely covered. Then just as quickly, pull your face out of the skillet and rush it back into the freezer for another five minutes. This will help the wax to set quicker. If you feel you want even more protection, feel free to repeat these steps again. The wax should help to protect your makeup from sweatin' off, but I still would make sure and find an air-conditionin' vent or unit to blow onto your face as often as possible. Good luck with Mr. Right. And I'll be lookin' for those tickets in the mail.

Love, Kisses, and Trailer Park Wishes,
Ruby Ann Boxcar

# Chapter 3

# Decoratin' the Trailer Park Way

*Our newest neighbor with the RV parked in Lot #20, coworker at the Blue Whale Strip Club with my sister Donna Sue, and owner of the floatin' Beauty Barge hair salon, Little Linda, who happens to be the only person in the park that would wear a black velvet sweater in August, shows off one of her pride and joys to visitor Flora Delight before they head off to dance at the Blue Whale. Not only is her oil rain lamp a decoration that would appease the eye in any trailer or RV, but when her Fry Daddy goes on the blink and she happens to be in the mood for onion rings or friend cheese sticks, all she has to do is put a stronger watt lightbulb in.*

You know, I got to tell y'all that I am proud to be trailer trash. Now, I know that some folks think that term is just degradin' and terrible, but you got to look at where it came from in order to understand why I love it so much. Trailer folks got that name on account of the fact that lots of us don't like to throw anythin' away, which is true. Of course we throw old food away, unless it happens to be macaroni or other pastas, which we dry out and use for decoratin'. But we keep practically everythin' else and reuse it. Of course we wouldn't take an old milk carton and fill it back up with milk or anythin' like that. That ain't the kind of reusin' I'm talkin' about at all. No, we'd just use it to make candles or create a decorative holder for all our loose change.

Trailer folks were actually the first true recyclists in the world, if you want to be honest. You're gonna find out in this chapter just how true that statement is. I'm gonna take items that you most likely never would have ever thought of reusin', and turn 'em into beautiful adornments for your home. Now I know that some of y'all will say, "Oh my goodness, how tacky is that," when you see some of the things that we're about to make. And that's fine, 'cause I know not everyone was as lucky as me to be brought up with an open mind and well-rounded taste when it comes to art and the finer things in life. But once you've made one of the followin' pieces, and have left it settin' around for a while, you'll notice just how stunningly beautiful it actually is. Why, I wouldn't be surprised if you don't start handin' these things out as presents for birthdays, weddin's, and even Christmas or Hanukkah to all your friends and family members. Yes, before long you'll be known all over town as that "person who gives your trash." The only thing I personally think that people could say about any of y'all that would be considered higher praise is, "Excuse me, but are you Ruby Ann Boxcar?"

Why, I remember back when I was just a little girl watchin' my momma make a kitchen dish-washin' sponge holder out of an empty detergent bottle. She added some scrap cloth and drawed on some eyes to make a funny little frog with a big cut-out mouth for the sponge to set in. Not only was it cute and clever, but it was also a way to save our planet, even though we didn't know that back then.

So the next time someone calls you trailer trash, just pop that old nose of yours up in the air, look 'em straight in the eye (even if it is hard to do both those things at the same time), and proudly tell 'em, "You're darn tootin' I am!"

Now, since some of y'all are new to the trailer life, I thought I'd take the time to introduce you and even instruct you in a few fun crafts so that you can get a jump on decoratin' your trailer. Since my holiday book has really caught on and more and more people are celebratin' all year round, you never know, unless you got a copy, when folks might surprise you and stop by to party on one of these year-round holidays. The last thing you want is someone to come by and get a look at the inside of your trailer home without any kind of handmade decorations in it. How embarrassin' would that be? Well, not to worry, 'cause we'll have you full-time trailer trash in no time.

I've also come to know durin' my recent travels many wonderful folks who are either in college or goin' off to college, and these kids have told me that they're stuck in these dorm rooms even though they wished they, too, could make their home a trailer. Well, I tell these fine outstandin' young adults not to worry 'cause it only takes one of these wonderful trailer-park-approved crafts beautifully displayed in their dorm room to bring my world of real good livin' to 'em. And this is also true for all you folks who for some reason or another are forced to live in an apartment, condo, town house, penthouse, skyscraper, office, box, or even a simple home. Don't let that stop you from livin' good. Why, when I'm on the road goin' from hotel room to hotel room I always make sure to bring some craft item with me just to keep me grounded as well as to remind me of what I get to go back to when I'm finished on that trip. Needless to say, it's always comfortin' to wake up in the middle of the night, not knowin' where I am, to see that macaroni-and-cheese picture frame with my husband, Dew's photo in it right there on the dresser. So grab your creative hat and clean off the kitchen table, 'cause it's time to decorate the old homestead.

## Skoal Can Candle

These beautiful decorative candles are sure to light up any trailer home, especially when they're lit. Finally your husband or wife can make up for all those accidentally spilled spit cups and stains on the carpet by donatin' their old discarded cans to this project. Not only do these do wonders for your trailer, but imagine how thrilled one of your family members or close friends will be when they find out that the present you brought for them contains a set of these stunnin' candles.

**Supplies**

Skoal can
Aluminum foil, cut down till it's 6 x 6 inches
Regular glue or hot glue
Scissors
Candle wax (enough to fill one can)
Wick with the self-centerin' tab attached to it

**1.** Start off by washin' out the inside of your Skoal can thoroughly with soap and water, makin' sure that you don't actually submerge the can. Set it aside and let it dry out completely overnight.

**2.** Next, you're gonna take a piece of aluminum and place it inside the can. Make sure that the bottom and insides are completely covered with aluminum. Once you've formed the aluminum to the inside of the can, carefully separate the aluminum from the can. Gently set the aluminum to the side.

**3.** Add a few drops of glue or a couple of shots of hot glue to the inside bottom of the can. Follow this by placin' the shaped foil back into the can. Make sure you press it down along the bottom and the sides real good.

**4.** Take your scissors and trim all the excess foil off so that it lays evenly along the top of the can.

**5.** Follow the instructions that came with the candle wax for preparation. Feel free to use any color of wax that you like. When the wax is ready, take your free-standin' wick and dip the tab that holds it straight up in and out of the wax. This should put a little wax on the tab. Now place the wick down into the middle of the foil-lined Skoal can. Press it down good and let it dry for a minute. This will help to keep the wick in place when you add the wax.

**6.** Slowly spoon in the wax until you get almost to the rim or top of the can. Let it cool down overnight. When the candle wax is hardened, place the tin cap on and set aside until you're ready to use. When the candle is not in use, place the tin back on the can. Not only is the candle cute with the top on, but it'll drive the Skoal user crazy when he keeps accidentally pickin' up the candle and puttin' it in his back pocket before headin' out the front door.

# Bingo Card Tissue Box Cover

Regardless if you're a winner or not, nothin' is quite as attractive as a bingo card tissue box cover made by your very own hand. Not only does this one-of-a-kind item show your creative side, but it also lets your guests know that you're one serious player. But most important, it helps to set the tone in your home regardless if you put it on the livin' room table or on the back of the commode in your guest bathroom. And of course, the vivid colors from both the cards and the dauber are sure to go with any color scheme you might have playin' out in your humble abode. Yes, the only downfall or bad part of this handy-dandy item is the demand you'll have from guests to make one for them. Oh, the pain of bein' crafty!

**SUPPLIES**

4 used bingo cards, which you've had laminated
Piece of cardboard (10.5 x 9.5 inches)
Pencil
Scissors
Hot glue
Empty tissue box
Spray paint, your choice of color
One of the followin':
    4 bingo bus passes

4 empty bingo daubers
13 bingo dauber tops

**1.** Take one of your bingo cards and lay it out on the cardboard. Trace around it on four different sections, and then set the card aside. Now, your pieces that you just traced out on the cardboard have got to be at least 5¼ inches tall as well as 4¾ inches wide, in order for them to fit over the tissue box. If your bingo cards ain't quite that big or they're a little bigger, then you can do one of two things. You can either take your bingo cards to a print shop and have 'em make you a copy of each card to those dimensions, or you can just go on ahead and use whatever cards you got as long as your cardboard pieces are as big as I've mentioned. If your bingo cards are a lot taller than 5¼ inches, then all you got to do when you've finished your cover is to put your tissue box in first and then put some wrinkled-up newspaper shoved up under it. This'll make your tissue box stay at the top of your large cover and look just as nice.

**2.** Cut out the pieces of traced cardboard. These will make your walls for the cover. Go ahead and assign and write a letter on each of the pieces starting with **A** and endin' with **D**. From now on we'll refer to each of these pieces by their letter.

**3.** We're gonna get an idea of how to glue these pieces together by simply lookin' at how each piece should fit. We will start off with pieces **A** and **B**. As you can see in the illustration below, the left end of **B** will be glued to the back right side of **A**, and the right end of **C** will be glued to the back left side of **A**. Then you simply put a little hot glue on the open ends of **B** and **C**, and stick on piece **D** to finish your four-walled rectangle.

**4.** Place either the top or the bottom open end on the cardboard and trace around it. This piece, which we will call **E**, will be the top piece for the rectangle. Cut it out, put hot glue along the top of pieces **A**, **B**, **C**, and **D**, and place piece **E** on top of them. You have now created your basic tissue-box-cover frame.

**5.** Take the empty tissue box and cut the top off of it. Set the top of the box on top of your rectangle. Make sure that it's centered, and then take your pencil and trace around the oval openin' of the tissue box top on piece **E**. That'll help you to make sure that your cover's openin' is just the right size. Discard the tissue box top, and go ahead and cut the traced oval out of **E**. If you find that the scissors are hard to work with on this part, feel free to use a box cutter or even a single-edge razor blade. Discard the oval when you've finished cuttin' it out.

**6.** Place your rectangle on a piece of newspaper and spray-paint it, makin' sure to get the inside edges where you just cut out the oval. Set it aside to dry.

**7.** When the box is dry, go ahead and put hot glue all along the inside edges of one of your bingo cards. Quickly place the card on one of the sides of the rectangle. Make sure you press the card on firmly and hold it in place until the glue has cooled. Repeat this until all sides of your rectangle are covered.

**8.** Next you will want to glue your bingo bus passes, dauber tops, or your empty daubers, on the top of the rectangle. If you used the dauber tops, just put a little hot glue on the top and press your tops into that. If you used your daubers, simply line 'em up on their sides end to end. Once you've finished the tissue box cover, give it a minute to dry, and then simply place it over a new open box of tissues. Put it out so everyone can see it.

# Macaroni-and-Cheese Picture Frame

Sure, when we was little we all made a macaroni frame, but I know it wasn't nothin' like this. Those old childhood frames, which brought a tear to many a mother's eyes, were beautiful, but most likely not somethin' that your momma would've actually left out in the livin' room. But our macaroni-and-cheese creation will be sure to look good in any room of the trailer. As a matter of fact, you're gonna find that all your guests will want to know where you got it. I always pretend to act real uppity and tell 'em that it was flown in all the way from Taiwan.

By the way, we're gonna start off by makin' a small 5 x 7-inch frame, but once you've mastered this size, there's no reason that you can't go on to the bigger ones, especially when you consider the cost of macaroni and cheese.

**SUPPLIES**

5" x 7" wooden picture frame
Newspaper
Can of white spray paint
Fan
Box of macaroni and cheese

Bottle of white glue
Paintbrush
Yellow food colorin'
Can of spray-on polyurethane

**1.** Take your clean wooden frame, place it on a piece of old newspaper, on its back, and give it a nice coat of white spray paint. Set this in front of a fan so it can dry faster.

**2.** Cook up your macaroni and cheese just like the instructions say. Set it aside, but don't let it cool down.

**3.** Once the frame has dried, leave it on the newspaper and take your glue and paintbrush and brush a nice layer of the glue all over the front and the sides of the dry frame.

**4.** Carefully spoon the warm macaroni and cheese on top of the areas containin' glue. Make sure that you get plenty on the sides as well. Gently press down to make sure that all of the macaroni is touchin' the frame. Set in front of the fan to dry (30 minutes to an hour).

**5.** Take the rest of the glue and add just a little water to slightly dilute it. Divide the glue into two portions. Take a few drops of yellow food colorin' and add it to one of the portions. Stir this up real good, put some plastic wrap over the top, and set it aside.

**6.** After the frame has dried, take the white glue and brush it onto the macaroni and cheese and the frame. Set it under the fan and let it dry completely before movin' on. This could take hours. Just check it every so often.

**7.** Next carefully lift the frame off of the newspaper and hold it up at an 80-degree angle. Take the yellow glue and, startin' from the top of the frame, brush it on the macaroni and cheese so that it looks like a cheese sauce. Feel free to skip some of the area so that it looks like you've poured it on. Place the frame at that angle, in front of the fan and let it set until it dries.

**8.** Once everythin' on the frame has completely dried, give it a good coat on the front, sides, and this time even on the back with the polyurethane. Wait just a bit and give it one more coat all over for luck.

**9.** When it has dried real good, take the glass, photo, and frame backin' and insert 'em. Place the frame anywhere you want in your home. Just remember to check it every once in a while since it does tend to sometimes get a little moldy as the months go by.

## Cigarette Tree

This is my tenth year of makin' cigarette trees, and I got to tell you that even though the number of smokers in the United States has gone down, the popularity of my cigarette trees has gone way up. I started off makin' 'em just for Christmastime as gifts, but now I make 'em all year round. Trust me when I tell you that once your guests see your handcrafted tree, you'll be the talk of the trailer park.

Now, there are two ways you can do your tree. You can either use old smoked butts or you can go out and buy some cheap smokes and simply tear the butts off. Since neither me or my husband, Dew, smoke no more, I've turned to my dear old sainted chimney smokin' mother-in-law, Momma Ballzak, for my butts. Around October I give her a Christmas red lipstick and ask her to wear it when she smokes. She empties her ashtrays out into a paper sack, and come November I start sortin' through those sacks, pickin' out graduated-size lipstick-stained butts for my trees.

Since my trees ain't always seasonal, I also create cigarette trees with unlipsticked butts and spray paint 'em green, red, blue, or any other color that I happen to like. This way I can keep displayin'my trees regardless of what the month might be. Of course I do have special trees that I put out just for the holidays. For example, I got one that I painted red, white, and blue that comes out for Flag Day, Presidents' Day, and Independence Day, and then there's my orange one with a small photo of Momma Ballzak on top of it for Halloween/Mother-in-Law's Day. So use your imagination, and remember that cigarette trees ain't just for Christmas anymore, so have fun with 'em. Oh, and by the way, if you don't want the smell of cigarettes in your house, but you do want the beauty that only a gorgeous cigarette tree can add, just give the butts a good once-over with some Febreeze before you start usin' 'em. Just make sure that you've let 'em dry before you stick 'em on to the Styrofoam cone.

**Supplies**

Tube of Styrofoam glue—any size will work, but I like the ones that are about 14" tall with a base that is around 4" wide.
White Styrofoam cone ($14\frac{7}{8}$ x $3\frac{7}{8}$ inches or larger)
Cigarette butts—amount depends on the size of your cone
Tree topper (optional)
Styrofoam ball—size is up to you (optional)
Bottle of white glue (optional)
Tube of gold glitter (optional)
Spray paint (optional)
Can of polyurethane spray

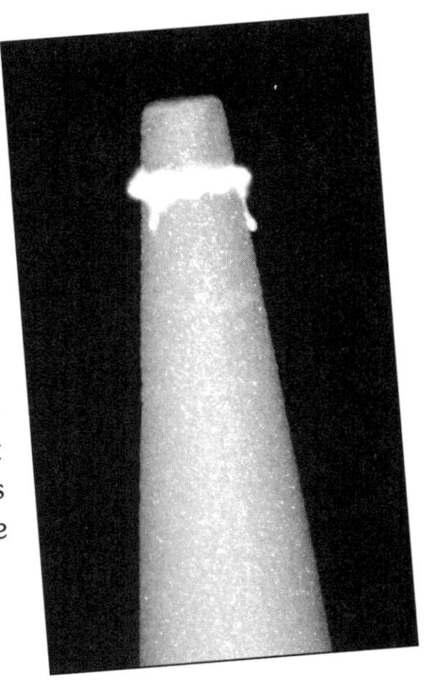

**1.** Take your glue and, startin' from $\frac{1}{4}$ inch down from the very top of the Styrofoam cone, apply one line of glue around the cone. Set your glue aside.

**2.** Next, take your first cigarette butt and with the burnt side facin' down, place it on the cone with the lipstick or filter side risin' slightly above the top of the cone. Press hard to make sure it sticks. Hold it for a second and then repeat until the butts make a crown goin' all the way around the top of the cone.

**3.** Go down about ¼ inch from the burnt end of the cigarette and put another line around the cone.

**4.** Place your next butt on this second line so that the filter side of the second line is touchin' the burnt end of the first line. Continue addin' the butts until the second line is complete.

**5.** Repeat steps 3 and 4 until you've reached the next-to-the-last row of butts at the bottom.

**6.** Now take a look at the space left on the bottom of the cone and figure out how long your last row of butts needs to be. Trim the butts down to that size.

**7.** Glue the last butts on to the cone. Set aside to dry.

**8.** When it comes to toppin' the tree, you can use either a Styrofoam ball or a lightweight turkey piece, or even a photo, dependin' on what the tree is for. Just glue it to the empty space at the top of the tree. But for the time bein', let's imagine that we are goin' to put a ball at the top.

**9.** Give the ball an even layer of glue. Roll it in the gold glitter. Gently set it aside to dry. If one of the sides that the ball was

dryin' on gets a bit messed up, just give it a shot of adhesive spray and resprinkle that area.

**10.** Next add a good amount of glue to the bare top of your cone and place the ball there. Make sure when you press down on the ball that you do it gently so that you don't knock off the glued butts.

**11.** If you want to spray-paint your tree, you can either do it before you put your toppin' on, if you want the tree and the toppin' to be a different color, or you can spray it afterwards.

**12.** Give the whole thing a light coatin' of polyurethane for safekeepin'.

## Elvis Shrine

Bein' the star that I am, I find that lately I'm spendin' lots of time on the road. Mind you, I ain't in no way complainin', especially since it means I get to meet and greet y'all in person. But to be honest, I do miss my trailer park surroundin's. And I know, from all the cards, letters, and e-mails that I get, that there're some of y'all out there who feel just like I do seein' how you've had to relocate on account of your husband or wife joinin' the military, gettin' transferred to a new job, or in a few cases, goin' off to college or work-related schools for a period of time. And to be plum darn honest, even though you're surrounded by regular folks, you still get lonely for that trailer park life. Well, let me tell you what I do to help fight the lack of good taste and bad decor that I find in these fancy, highfalutin' hotels they put me in. I bring a piece of the trailer park with me. That's right, regardless of where I go or how long I'm gonna be there, I've always got a place in my suitcase for what I call my little bit of heaven, my Elvis shrine. And, folks, let me tell y'all, I don't care how nice the room might be, nothin' will bring it down a notch and make it feel more like a mobile home than havin' this tribute to the King settin' on your hotel TV or nightstand. You can only imagine the comfort that a decorated mangled soda pop bottle can bring you. So now, regardless of how far away the closest trailer might be, you'll never be lonely for home when you got a lovely Elvis shrine settin' or even hangin' wherever you are. And the best part is that it's so easy to make, you'll be sharin' and enjoyin' the presence of the King in no time flat.

Even though you can never have enough Elvis items in your trailer home, there are some times when you might want to hang up decorations like this one, but with a different theme. I say that 'cause this Elvis shrine can also be changed slightly to a lovely bird decor by simply usin' different colors of paint and suspendin' a bird on a perch instead of a photo of Elvis. Or you could even go with a Christmas theme and put an old Christmas card inside the bottle and paint the outside green, red, or white. Since the only thing that can hold you back when it comes to changin' the subject matter of your soda pop bottle shrine is your imagination, anything is possible.

Before we get started, let me just tell y'all that regardless of how strong the desire might be to put a candle or two next to this shrine, be careful, 'cause it'll melt like a snowman in July. With that said, let's get ready to pay honor to the King of Rock and Roll.

### Supplies

- 2-liter plastic soda pop bottle, cleaned out, de-labeled, and de-glued
- Measurin' tape
- Black fine-point marker
- Electric wood-burnin' tool
- Gold acrylic paint
- Paintbrush
- 10 inches of fishin' line

Scissors
Fishin' swivel
Photo of Elvis, no bigger than 3 x 5 inches
3-inch wire
3 beads
White puff or dimensional paint
Cotter pin

**1.** With the bottle cap on, take a measurin' tape and, startin' at the cap, measure down 4 inches, and mark it with your fine-point marker. Next, take a piece of paper, the thicker the better, and wrap it clean around the bottle so that the paper remains even with itself and rests right under that mark that you made. This paper is gonna be your guide to how long 4 inches from the cap is all around the bottle. You will take your marker, put it at the mark you made on the bottle, and usin' the edge of the paper, draw a straight line all around the bottle until you've come back to that mark.

**2.** Take your measurin' tape and measure down 4¾ inches from that line that you just drew around the bottle. Mark it and use the paper again to draw a straight line goin' all around the bottom of the bottle exactly 4¾ inches from the top line.

**3.** Get your measurin' tape back out and run it around that top line. It should be around 13 inches long. Take your marker and mark every ½ inch on that line goin' around until you get to the place where you started. This should give you a total of 25 little marks all along that top line that you drew.

**4.** Now take your marker and go down to the bottom line. Tryin' to be as close as you can be, take the first ½-inch mark that you made on that top line and put a new mark directly below it on the bottom line. Go to the next ½-inch mark and do the same thing. When you're done, you should have ½-inch marks on

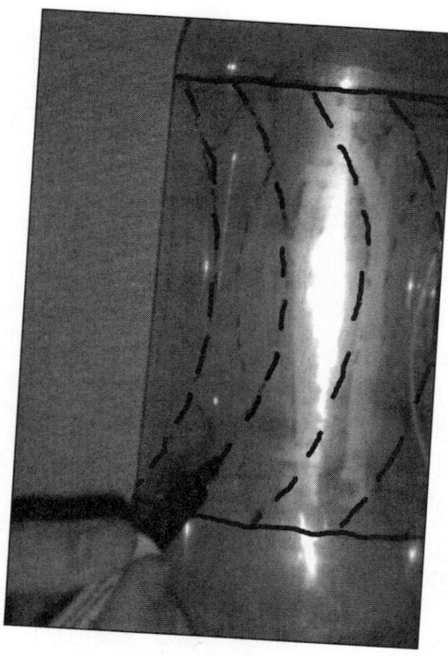

the top line and ½-inch marks on the bottle line directly below it as well.

**5.** Startin' from one of the marks on the top of the bottle, draw a bent or wavy line with your marker all the way down to the mark below it just like in the picture below. Do this to all the marks that you made.

**6.** Take your marker and draw a big E and a P between the cap section and the line at the top of the bottle that you drew. See the photo below. Draw a second E and P directly across on the other side of the bottle

**7.** Plug in your wood-burnin' tool, and when it's ready, take it and carefully cut on the E, makin' sure not to burn or cut out the three lines of the right of the E. We only want the left and the middle section of the E to be cut. The same is true for the P, but in this case, we only want to cut out the middle and right sections of the P. This way we can lift up the right of the E and the left of the P so that we have a 3-D effect. See the photo below to see what it should look like once you've finished cuttin' on the letters. Move over to the other set of letters and do the same thing.

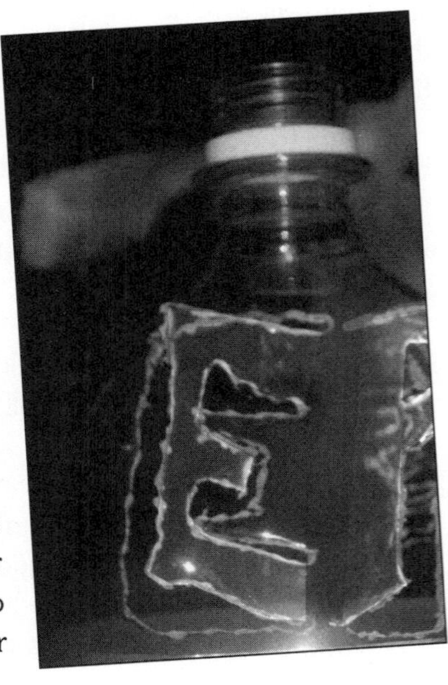

**8.** Take your wood-burnin' tool and follow the wavy or bent lines that you drew between the two lines all around the bottle. Set your tool aside, and bend out the cut lines. These are now gonna be referred to as your blades. They will allow you to peer into your bottle. Plus if you suspend your

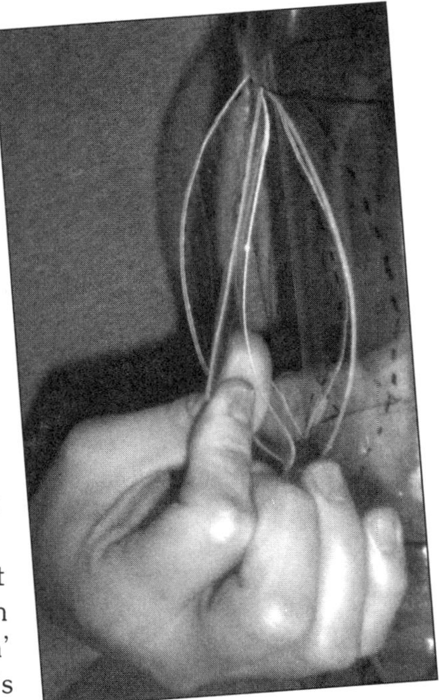

shrine from the ceilin', when your heat or air kicks on in the trailer or wherever you might be, the blades will catch that breeze and make your shrine spin just little.

**9.** Next you'll want to take your hot wood-burnin' tool and make two very small holes directly opposite of each other in the neck and one more real tiny hole right in the middle of the bottom of the bottle as well (that bottom hole should be just big enough for a piece of the fishin' line to go through). Unplug your tool and set it aside to cool off.

**10.** Take your gold paint and paint the top of the inside and the bottom part of the inside by carefully puttin' your paintbrush through the openin's between the blades. Just make sure that you don't actually paint the blades themselves. Set aside to dry.

**11.** You will need to punch a little hole at the top of your picture as well as one at the bottom. Tie a 4-inch piece of fishin' line to the top of the photo and a 6-inch piece of fishin' line to the bottom. Once you've tied the knots on the strings, take your scissors and make sure to clip the knots up real good so you ain't got no loose piece of fishin' line interferin' with the King's picture.

**12.** Take that top piece of fishin' line and tie it to the end of a fishin' swivel. There should be about 3 to 3½ inches of line between the photo and the swivel.

**13.** Place the photo of the King and the line and the swivel all inside the bottle via the blade openin's. Now you're gonna take that piece of wire and insert it into one of the neck holes that you made earlier. Run that wire through the other end of the fishin' swivel and out the other neck hole. This is much easier to do if the bottle is lyin' on its side.

**14.** Place a bead on the outside ends of the wire. Twist your wire ends so that the beads won't come off. Not only do the beads look pretty, but they help to hold the wire in place.

**15.** String the fishin' line that's tied to the bottom of the picture

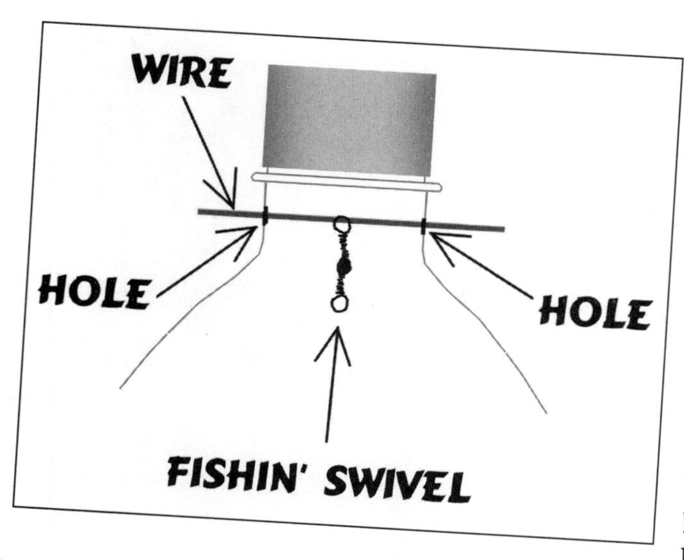


through the hole in the bottom of the bottle. Make sure it's nice and taut and tie a few knots in it so that the string won't slip back through the hole. You can also add a little dab of glue there to help cover up that hole. You should now have a suspended Elvis hangin' in your bottle.

**16.** Next grab your white puff paint and on the outside of the bottle, paint your E and P letters. Then go ahead and paint over both the black marker lines you made around the top and bottom parts of the bottle. You can also paint a thin line of puff paint along the outside of the blades where the black lines are that you drew on. Be creative, but make sure that there is still enough gold showin'. Set the bottle aside and let it dry completely. Your standin' shrine is now finished.

**17.** If you want to hang up your shrine, all you got to do is to punch a small hole in the bottle cap, run a cotter pin through a bead and then down into the hole, bend the ends of the cotter pin so that it can't come back out of the hole, string a piece of fishin' line through the cotter hole, tie the ends of the fishin' strings together to make a loop, and hang it up with pride.

# Gingerbread Trailer

Now, don't be fooled about the old myth that gingerbread buildin's are only for the holidays. That's a bunch of baloney that some lazy person came up with. You can make a gingerbread trailer any day of the week. And the best part is that once you've made it, unlike a gingerbread house, you ain't got to stand guard over it all night and day long. After all, if somebody takes a nibble off your gingerbread trailer, it'll just look like a twister came by and blew a part of it off into another county. So enjoy, but remember that this is a two-day project and there ain't no gettin' around that.

**SUPPLIES**

20 x 20-inch piece of plywood
20 x 20-inch piece of green wrappin' paper or green poster board
Foil
3 or 4 bakin' sheets
1 cup margarine, room temperature
1¾ cups brown sugar
1¼ cups white sugar
6 eggs
2 tablespoons molasses
6 cups all-purpose flour

2 teaspoons bakin' soda
1 tablespoon ground ginger
1 tablespoon ground cinnamon
1 tablespoon allspice
3 or 4 coolin' racks
Fruit roll-ups
Sugar cubes
Small toy car you don't need any longer

## Icin'

3 egg whites
1½ teaspoons cream of tartar
3 to 3½ cups icin' sugar
Can of decoratin' spray—this is to paint your trailer with so pick whatever color you like
2 or 3 cans of white decoratin' icin' with the decoratin' tips
Can of white decoratin' spray
Can of gray decoratin' spray
8 black Twizzlers or sticks of black licorice

**1.** Take the plywood and cover with green wrappin' paper or green poster board.

**2.** Cut out your pattern pieces from the cardboard. You'll need two 12 x 5-inch pieces to make the sides of the trailer, two 4 x 5-inch pieces to make the front and back of the trailer, one 12 x 4.5-inch piece to make the roof of the trailer, one 3 x 1.5-inch piece to use for doors, one 2 x 2-inch piece to use for the side window, and one 3 x 2-inch piece to use for the bay window at the very front of the trailer.

**3.** Preheat your oven to 325 degrees F.

**4.** Wrap foil around your bakin' sheets and then margarine 'em up and sprinkle on some flour.

**5.** Take a big bowl and cream the margarine and both brown and white sugars together. Then beat in your eggs and your molasses. Set aside.

**6.** In another big bowl, sift your flour, bakin' soda, ginger, cinnamon, and allspice together. Combine both mixtures well and then knead 'em into a smooth ball. Cover and put in the fridge for 45 minutes.

**7.** Flour down a flat surface and roll out your dough until it's about 1/4 inch thick.

**8.** Lay your first five large cardboard pattern pieces on top of the gingerbread and carefully cut them out. Then take one of the 12 x 5-inch cut-out gingerbread pieces and cut out the window. You will also want to cut out a door on that same piece, but just remember to cut your door up high towards the top of the piece so we can build stairs comin' up to our gingerbread entrance. Next take the other 12 x 5-inch cut-out gingerbread piece and cut out a door on it as well, rememberin' to cut it up high on the piece. Finally take one of the 4 x 5-inch cut-out gingerbread pieces and cut out the bay window from it. Make sure you put the doors and windows carefully on a bakin' sheet along with the five large pieces. You might want to use a spatula to help you get the pieces on the bakin' sheets.

**9.** Place your cut pieces in the oven and bake for 15 to 20 minutes.

**10.** Next you need to form a base for the gingerbread to rest on, and you do this by duct-tapin' your cardboard pattern pieces together in the shape of the trailer. The 12 x 5-inch pieces will be the long sides of the trailer with the 4 x 5-inch pieces bein' used as the front and the back of your finished gingerbread mobile home. After you've taped those together, you'll want to place your 12 x 4.5-inch piece on top for your trailer roof. When you've duct-taped the whole thing together, you should have a perfect rectangular box to use as your base.

**11.** Take the gingerbread out of the oven and shut it off. Undo the foil from the sides of the bakin' sheets. With the gingerbread still on the foil, transfer the foil from the bakin' sheets to the racks. Let 'em cool overnight.

**12.** Mix up icin' glue. Beat egg whites till they foam. Add the cream of tarter, beat till whites are stiff. Slowly add icin' sugar and beat for 5 minutes. Keep it in fridge till needed.

**13.** Take the icin' glue and, startin' with the front of the trailer, put a thick layer of icin' directly on the cardboard.

**14.** Take the matchin' gingerbread piece and carefully apply a layer of icin' glue to the back of it, then gently press it against the iced portion of the trailer where the piece belongs.

**15.** Repeat steps 13 and 14 with each side, front, and roof piece, makin' sure to have plenty of icin' glue where the pieces touch. Don't worry if your corner icin' glue shows. After all, this is just for decoration, and you ain't got to live in it. Just give the whole thing 30 minutes to dry before movin' on to the next step.

**16.** Take your decoratin' spray, you've selected the color of this one, and spray down the entire trailer.

**17.** Next we will make the trailer skirtin' by applyin' white icin' from a decoratin' can. Choose your favorite decoratin' tip and put it on the can dispenser. Draw an icin' line across the trailer that runs from the bottom of your door and all around your trailer. Then just apply the icin' below the lines on all the trailer sides until you have a fun trailer skirt.

**18.** Take a piece of fruit roll-up that you've cut out to be 2 x 2 inches. Put some icin' glue on the back of it and stick it in your side window. These are your curtains. Ain't they beautiful?

**19.** Take the fruit-roll up that you've cut out to be 3 x 2 inches and slap some icin' on the back of this one as well. This is your bay window curtain. Place it into the cut-out hole on the front of the trailer.

**20.** It's time to make the stairs. Take your sugar cubes and on the side of your trailer in front of your door hole stack one whole row up until you get almost to the bottom of the door. You should have a row goin' straight across from one side of the door to the other with sugar cubes stacked up to the door hole. Next stack some more cubes up in front of those, but make that stack one cube shorter than the first stack. Make another line of stacked sugar cubes two cubes shorter, and keep doin' this until you are down to a row that goes straight across that is only one cube high. See the photo next door to get a better idea of how these should look.

**21.** Take a piece of paper and put it between the back row of the sugar cubes and the trailer. Now carefully take your gray decoratin' spray and give a light coatin' to the sugar cube stairs that you just made. Carefully remove the paper when you've finished.

**22.** While you've got it out, go ahead and take out four sugar cubes and give each of 'em a nice coatin' with that gray decoratin' spray. Then set 'em aside for later.

**23.** Take your door pieces and spray 'em down with white decoratin' spray.

**24.** Cut your 2 x 2-inch window piece and cut it straight down the middle so you have two 1 x 2-inch pieces. Spray these white as well with the decoratin' spray.

**25.** Startin' with the back door, which has no steps, by the way, you want to take that door piece and put a thick coat of icin' glue on the unsprayed side. Stick the door in the empty door hole. If it don't fit, carefully trim it down till it does.

**26.** Movin' to the side of your trailer that has a window and a door, take a tube of black icin' and color in the empty door area.

**27.** Put icin' glue on the left inside of the door hole. Next take your remainin' door and press the left corner of it into the icin' glue, allowing the right corner of the door to rest on the sugar cube stairs. This will make it look like your door is cracked open welcomin' all guests, with the exception of bill collectors and Jehovah Witnesses.

**28.** Take your 1 x 2-inch pieces that were once your window and slap some icin' glue on the back of those. These will serve as your window shutters, so place one on each side of the window.

**29.** Now take the can of the white decoratin' icin' and run a straight line completely around the top of the trailer. This is your trailer trim. Also run trim or frames of the white decoratin' icin' around your windows and doors.

**30.** Take your Twizzlers or sticks of licorice and roll each up tightly to form a tire that measures 1½ inches across. Add a toothpick to hold it together and camouflage the toothpick areas that show with black icin' from the tube. Place the tires on top of the trailer roof.

**31.** Take a toy car and carefully break the tires off of it. Discard the tires. Place the four gray sugar cubes that you painted earlier on the green paper and put the car on top of those. Now you have your car up on edible cinder blocks.

**32.** Decorate your yard with miniature TV's, washin' machines, cans or bottles, newspapers, flamingos, or other fun little items. Just be creative.

Now that y'all have an idea of what you can do to make your trailer a thing of beauty, go ahead and get started. Feel free to try to do anything. Be like my sister who took all them empty Crisco cans that she had lyin' around her trailer and turned 'em into planters and candle holders. Go ahead and be inventive like my Me-Ma who took a broken ice tea jar and a bunch of empty toilet paper rolls and made binoculars for children (don't worry, we got her back into the home). The important thing is to simply be yourself when you decorate around the trailer. Just remember that regardless of what others say, either to your face or behind your back—and they will talk—in the end you and yours are the ones who have to live with it. So you might as well live in full trailer park style.

## Ask Ruby Ann . . .

Dear Ruby Ann,

I've thrown myself into a deep pit of depression that only you can help me get out of. I take personal pride in the way my living room looks, which is why I've put only the best decorations in it. I have a lovely coffee table that my husband made for me out of wood and wrought iron, and on top of that I got my two-and-a-half-foot hand-painted ceramic matador on one end and my just-as-large orange ceramic bull on the other. Velvet paintings of both Elvis and John Wayne as well as some beautiful selections of string art cover my walls, along with family photos in frames that I've personally covered with that neon fake fur. I got them beautiful air fresheners in every unused electrical outlet in the room. And of course my plastic revolvin' fireplace log is plugged in year-round. But the part that just has driven me into utter insanity is that for some odd reason my rain lamp has stopped workin' correctly. Some of the strings no longer have drops of oil runnin' down 'em, causin' it to just look tacky. I've called everywhere and talked to everyone I could think of until I was blue in the face tryin' to find someone that works on rain lamps. I know you'll find this hard to believe, but not one person in Lawton repairs rain lamps. And, Ruby Ann, I just don't know what to do! I had to take it down from the ceilin', and my livin' room just looks off somehow. Even my husband, when he takes a break from playin' his Atari on the TV, makes comments about how weird the livin' room looks without the rain lamp. I tried takin' the swag lamp out of the bedroom and hangin' it up in the same place where the rain lamp was, but it didn't look right at all. I'm so embarrassed to entertain company because of this, and when someone does stop by unexpected, as soon as they've come through the door I try to draw their attention away by handin' them a talking View-Master to enjoy. Ruby Ann, please help me.

Tillie
Lawton, Oklahoma

Dear Tillie,

Oh my goodness, dear, how are you gettin' by? I just can't imagine. Thank goodness we got a fella just down the road who specializes in rain lamp repair. As a matter of fact, that and motion lamps are about all he works on, which explains why he's busy all the time. With that said, let me just tell you that I got good news, I can help. After givin' Zeb a call at his shop, he came to the conclusion that what's most like your problem is that your holes where the oil drips out from are clogged. Zeb says that he sees this kind of thing all the time from dust and such. What you need to do is take a toothpick and shove it up your holes. That should do the trick for you right there. Zeb did tell me to just remind you to make sure and give your lamp a good cleanin' at least once a week in order to keep it from cloggin' on you. Oh, and he said that you might want to also add a little more mineral oil to your lamp and take a chunk of paraffin wax to the strings. He says this will make that rain lamp flow like Niagara Falls. I hope this helps.

By the way, I'd sure love to see your home when I pass through Lawton one day. From the sound of it, you got quite the showplace. And my husband, Dew, was wonderin' if maybe your husband might be up for a game or two of Pong. When he ain't out fishin', he's on playin' that Pong thing like there's no tomorrow.

Love, Kisses, and Trailer Park Wishes,
Ruby Ann Boxcar

# Chapter 4

# Trailer Park-Style Entertainin'

*Fun and games are always enjoyable at any gatherin' you might hostess at, but you know the party is just about over when your sister's new boyfriend duct-tapes your good Family Dollar wall clock or his wristwatch to his head and introduces himself as her new antique grandfather clock.*

I don't know if it's my warm personality or just my gift of gab, but ask anyone who's ever been over to my trailer and they'll tell y'all that I'm definitely the hostess with the mostess when it comes to fun. I just love to entertain guests regardless whether it's a simple gatherin' for cards or a nice all-out dinner party. Maybe I'm so good at hostessin' 'cause of my motherin' side, which has been trapped and muted on account of the fact that I had my tubes tied many years ago (I didn't want any children of mine to spend their lives feelin' like they had to try to compete with their mother or even live in my shadow). Or perhaps it's the fact that I'm a stickler for party-givin' protocol. I don't know, but I can tell you this, I've found on a firsthand basis that when I've been just a guest that the magic of entertainin' sure seems to be lackin'.

I actually attended a private dinner party not too long back and even though the hostess, who will remain nameless, was as sweet as can be and one of my favorite ladies of all time, she was sure missin' somethin' when it came to correctly entertainin'. God bless her, I know she's busy and all, but when we'd all sat down to eat, the only thing she had for a centerpiece was a napkin holder that someone had obviously gotten from a Denny's at one time or another. I have to tell y'all, I truly was disappointed. And I want y'all to know that I say this with true love and compassion, but, for goodness sakes, if you're gonna stand up and represent a wonderful state like New York in the senate, then the least you can do is find the time to hot-glue an assortment of rhinestones or even silk flowers on to the aluminum sides of that dang restaurant napkin holder when you know you've got company comin' over. Of course I'm sure she knows by now that she had made a entertainin' mistake. And I'm also sure that she'll never repeat it again unless of course somebody got into that guest bathroom before her and wiped off that message I'd written to her in lipstick on her mirror.

Luckily, when it comes to havin' guests over for dinner, just as long as you follow my helpful tips y'all ain't got to worry about those kinds of blunders. Why, I'm goin' to tell y'all how to set your table and even show you how to make napkin holders and place cards that are sure to impress your guests regardless of what side of the track they was born on. So grab your plates and get out your best penmanship, 'cause we're ready to prepare for a party.

## Formal or Informal

Now, this here is real easy to deal with on account of that no kind of gatherin', with the exception of some weddin's, in a trailer park is ever formal. As I'm sayin' that, I also want you to understand that not everythin' is informal either. We do have two different types of gatherin's—informal get-togethers and change your shirt get-togethers. Typically informal gatherin's are held outside or in the recreation room, which is better known as the rec room, or even down in the storm cellar. The change your shirt gatherin's, as you might have guessed, are normally the ones where you have to go over to someone's trailer or when attendin' special events in the park like say a Christmas party, when someone important like the mayor, a star, a sports legend, or Billy Graham will be in attendance, a Tupperware, Avon, Mary Kay, Amway, Shaklee, or any other kind of product demonstration party. So now, with all that in mind, let's see if you can answer the followin' question.

**Q.** ***If Pastor Ida Mae Bee invites you and everyone else to come on over to her trailer for a simple BBQ, which type of get-together is it?***

**a.** Informal
**b.** Change your shirt

**A.** Your clues to this were "BBQ," "everyone else," and "Pastor Ida May Bee." Yes, it is a large gatherin', and it will be held outside, which would normally mean informal, but since the pastor is gonna be in attendance, in this case the correct answer is *b*. Regardless if you are

Baptist or not, when a member of the cloth is present all the other rules are superseded, makin' the event a change your shirt get-together. The only time this ain't true is if the clergy is from one of them far-out groups like Moonies, Hare Krishnas, or Presbyterians.

## What to Wear

Since we're talkin' about a dinner in another person's trailer home, you'll want to put on clean clothes regardless of how much you might like or dislike the people you're about to dine with. Typically us trailer park gals will come over in a pair of our everyday double-knit polyester slacks, and some kind of blouse that ain't too revealin', and that's got sleeves of some kind so we ain't got to haul out the razor. And the menfolk will put on a pair of clean jeans or at least a pair that they ain't wore when they was workin' on the car or out fishin' in just before. And they'll change into a clean T-shirt that ain't got any kind of dirty or suggestive comments or photos on it. The big thing us married gals have to watch when it comes to our men is that they don't wear their muddy shoes to dinner. We make 'em put on their sneakers or somethin' that's clean. The important thing to remember when you dress for any kind of event is that you wear clothes that are right for the event, but still comfortable.

Oh, and one more thing, only pure gutter trash would wear a caftan outside their lot. Everybody with any kind of class or taste knows that a caftan is only to be worn when you're relaxin' around your trailer, goin' out to get your mail or newspaper, steppin' out to briefly pick up a lawn statue that's blown over, leanin' out of your trailer to yell at either your kids or strange little hoodlums that are in your yard, answerin' your door, or runnin' out to your truck to get somethin' you forgot. You never *ever* wear your caftan/muumuu when entertainin', goin' over to borrow a cup of sugar, climbin' up on top your roof to reposition your TV antenna or satellite dish, or to chase down the Schwan's truck. And no self-respectin' true trailer park dweller would be caught dead in a caftan in church, the grocery store, a restaurant, their car, someone else's car, the doctor or dentist's office, or for that matter, on TV. Now, there are only two exceptions to that TV thing, and they are if your trailer was just blown away by a twister or if *COPS* is filmin' the arrest of somebody in your trailer court and you ain't got time to change before they pack away their cameras and lights and load up the police car to leave.

So let's try another question to see if you're gettin' this yet. Since I've talked about both the right way for women and men to dress, each answer will have both the female/male attire listed. Here comes the question.

**Q.** ***If it's Christmas mornin' and your family are comin' over to open presents with y'all, which should you be wearin'?***

- **a.** Slacks and a blouse/jeans and a clean T-shirt
- **b.** Caftan/old pants and an old T-shirt
- **c.** Housecoat/robe

**A.** I know that this one is a little harder, but you should have been able to get it. Even though you're havin' guests over, they're only your loved ones, so *a* would be too dressy. And since housecoats and robes tend to fly open from time to time, and your relatives will most likely dress up as much as you will, *c* is never an option. So in this case, *b* is correct. The reason for this is that it's mornin' on a holiday that you share with your family and it's in your trailer, so you should be relaxed and laid-back. Now if it was me goin' over to, say, my sister's trailer for Christmas or Thanksgivin', then I'd put on a nice pair of slacks and a blouse, but I'd bring along a caftan to change into when we got there. After all, with all the hard work I do, I want to be relaxed and laid-back as well on these holidays. Plus, if food is gonna be served, I ain't got to worry about them uncomfortable slacks. After all, my husband, Dew, along with the rest of the menfolk are just gonna undo their pants and zip down their zippers after they feast, so I might as well be comfortable around my own clan too.

One more little thing about the proper apparel in regard to the above question. At no time is it right for your husband to wear shorts when anyone, includin' your family, is over. Y'all can have a white Christmas without your husband's pasty white legs shinin' in front of everyone. Plus, there might be children present and you don't want his ivory limbs to scare 'em into terrible Christmas memories that they have to spend years in therapy tryin' to get over.

## Invitations

The only time paper invitations are used in a trailer park is when somebody's gettin' hitched. On all other occasions, invitations are always oral. You either call up the guests and invite 'em, tell 'em face-to-face, or after you chase their kids out of your yard or from under your trailer you tell 'em, "The next time you set your tiny little foot past that curb I'm gonna beat your behind into next week, so get your little hoodlum butt over to your trailer right now before I set my dogs loose, and tell your momma to come over for dinner next Tuesday at six!" This question's easier.

**Q.** ***If you decide to go ahead and throw a dinner party for those who'll be helpin' out with your daughter's weddin' next week to her boyfriend that's currently in jail for solicitation to an undercover police officer till his folks can come up with bail money, how should you ask 'em?***

**a.** Send out invitations
**b.** Do oral invitations

**A.** Now, even though a weddin' is involved, we're talkin' about a dinner where those folks who will be participatin' in the weddin' will be the guests. In this case, the correct answer is *b*. And since you don't know if the groom will be hungry or not when he gets out of jail, don't put the dinner off on his account. Simply call up your guests and tell 'em when to come over and whether they need to bring their own TV trays or not.

## Greetin' the Arrivin' Guests

Actually this section should be broken down into two parts, which are "Greetin' the Invited Guests" and "Greetin' the Uninvited Guests." So, let's start off with the latter if y'all don't mind.

How many times have you got everythin' in the oven cookin' like a crazy lady when the doorbell rings. You answer it only to find one of your neighbors who got a wild hair up their behind to drop by for a social visit. You don't want to be rude, yet you still got to set the table. What do you do? It's easy. If the bell ringer is someone that your guests will enjoy bein' around, simply give the neighbor two choices. Tell 'em that you're so glad to see 'em, but you're busy 'cause you got people comin' over for dinner. Make sure the bell ringer knows who the people are before you get to the two-choices part. After you've said all this, you will then add the followin', "So I'm either gonna have to let you go, dear, or if you want to stay you're gonna have to go to the Colonel's and pick up some chicken 'cause I ain't got enough food for all of us." Now, notice how you don't tell 'em that they can just come in and hang out without eatin'. No, you've told 'em that they can stay as long as they pick up some chicken from KFC. So if they come back with the line about how they'll just set in the livin' room while y'all eat, set 'em straight. Tell 'em that won't work, because "us eatin' with you in the other room will make my guests as well as me and my husband feel uncomfortable, so again, if you want to come in and stay, then you first need to go hit the drive-thru at the Colonel's." Now it's up to the uninvited guest to decide whether to stay.

If the uninvited guest decides to go pick up some chicken, make sure he knows what to get. Stop him before he heads out and say, "Don't come back here with an eight-piece dinner and think I'm gonna let you in. You know that won't feed no more than one adult and a child. Bring back the big bucket, and make sure you got sides. Don't even think about ringin' the doorbell again if you ain't got a big side of coleslaw and a tub of mashed potatoes and gravy in your bag. And don't forget the extra biscuits." Be firm and let 'em know that if they want to join the party then they got to pay to get in.

Now if the person at the door is somebody that you really don't want over durin' dinner, just tell 'em that you've got some guests comin' over for a prayer group/foot anointin' service. Trust me when I tell y'all that if the first part don't make 'em leave, then the foot anointin' will. Nobody, but nobody, wants to be in a trailer full of people who've taken off their shoes, regardless if it is for a religious purpose. The reason for this is not that we ain't clean or nothin', but we just love our shoes. We love our shoes so much that we wear the same one or two pairs all the time until either they fall apart or the duct tape just won't hold no more. In any case, they get a workout, which means they have very little time to air out and such. So the last thing you want to attend is a foot anointin' in a small trailer home. If this excuse don't work, then just tell 'em that you're havin' Mexican food and you want to be able to enjoy it. Follow this by closin' the door. This should do the trick.

When your invited guests arrive, you should welcome 'em in with open arms. Most likely you'll be runnin' late with somethin', so tell 'em to take a seat in the livin' room. You'll already have the TV on and your husband will probably already be settin' in there so he can make small talk with 'em. If your guests ask if they can help with anything in the kitchen, tell them thanks, but that you've got everythin' covered. You don't need some person addin' stuff and messin' up the meal you've been slavin' over that hot stove all day long to make.

Feel free to offer 'em a sweet tea or a soda pop. Never tell your guests to help themselves to anythin' in the kitchen when you ain't around. The last thing you want 'em to do is either stumble across your booze stash or help themselves to a beer. The reason for this is the same reason that you don't offer your guests a beer or alcoholic drink when they first arrive. If they think they're gonna be able to get a beer or cocktail when they arrive, you'll have 'em at your door thirty minutes to an hour before they're supposed to be there, and you don't need that. As a matter of fact, I never serve adult beverages of any kind to my guests when they come over just for the simple fact that you don't know how folks will act when they happen to tie one on. Now, I can already hear some of y'all sayin' how one little drink ain't gonna hurt nobody, but that just ain't true. Some folks like myself ain't got to drink more than one cocktail or beer to get hammered. We are what my sister calls lightweights. Now, I just get more entertainin' when I'm sauced, but some folks get down right hateful, so I say no booze when you come to visit. After all, the last thing I want to do is have to throw your mean-spirited drunken butt out of my trailer.

If you happen to be the invited guest that is arrivin', there are a few things that you need to remember before knockin' on the door.

**1.** Never bring your purse or a bag in with you. You surely don't want to accidentally bring roaches back home in your purse or bag. So lock your purse in your trunk before goin' in for dinner.

**2.** When you arrive, always ask if there is anythin' in the kitchen that you can help out with. This is your chance to add some kind of flavor to that bland food that your hostess tends to be known around the trailer park for.

**3.** Have an escape planned with your husband or wife just in case you walk into the trailer and it smells. I don't care how nice these people might be, the worst thing in the world is to be trapped inside a trailer that stinks. I've always found that the best medicine for this is to bring a gift of three or four of those special candles that kill odors with me for the hostess. Of course I tear off or mark over with a black marker the section on the package that says anythin' about killin' bad odors. After all, I ain't heartless. I make sure to keep a few extras in my trunk just in case the ones I brung in ain't quite doin' the job. But if you still can't stand the smell, and know you won't be able to eat unless you're right next to an open window, then have some plan worked out with your mate that will get you out of that trailer earlier than planned. I just send my husband out for my eyeglass cleaner when I got to leave early. He knows that this is his signal to go outside and call me from his cell phone. When my bra starts ringin', which is where I carry my phone when my purse is locked up in the trunk, I answer it and pretend that it's somethin' major that requires us to leave. When my husband, Dew, comes back into the trailer, I tell him about the call and that we got to rush. We give our best and get the heck out that stench hole.

**4.** When you're invited to take a seat in the livin' room, never take the host's or hostess's chair. That is rude. If you don't know which chair is the host's or hostess's seat, simply look for the ones that have been clearly marked by the hostess with a paper sign that reads DON'T SIT HERE!

**5.** If you like a specific drink like, say, caffeine-free diet Coke, then make sure you bring a bottle or two of it with you. Your hostess might not keep that in stock, so grab some, write your name on it in big letters, put it in a bag, and bring it along. When you arrive, just say that you brought a little gift and give it to the hostess. At dinnertime, when she asks you what you want to drink tell her. You know she'll have it. And at the end of the night when you get ready to leave, just grab whatever is left. Don't take the bag that you brought them in, however (remember, roaches).

## How to Set Your Table

As y'all can guess just by the way I handle myself, I've been the guest at many social events. Of course, bein' the expert that I am on proper etiquette and all, I must make some folks feel uncomfortable, 'cause I'm rarely invited back. But this is not the case when it comes to trailer park events. Folks whose homes have wheels just love to have me over and often. I think it's on account of the fact that we're much more conscious with the ways of etiquette than those who don't live in mobile homes, and so our dinner experience is much more at ease. An example of this is how were set our tables for these big shindigs.

I can't tell you how many times I've gone to a non-trailer dinner only to notice that the folks who'd set up and cleaned off the area where I was seated for dinner counted the forks, spoons, knives, and other utensils I'd used. I know this was to make sure that they'd given me the right number to start off with and then when I got up from the table they wanted to just double-check themselves. Obviously these folks had not entertained very much, or at least they hadn't had others who were as well-groomed as I am to dinner on a regular basis. You could just tell by the way they acted around me that they were watchin' everythin' I did in an attempt to copy my highly polished correctness. This is somethin' that doesn't happen in trailer homes. Nobody there is afraid of slippin' up or makin' a social blunder, 'cause our mommas brung us up to know how to act around company. These skills show in every aspect, but none as much as the way we set our dinner table for company.

The first thing we got to do when it comes to settin' our table is to prepare it. We do this by takin' everythin' off of it and givin' it a good wipe-down with a damp sponge or hand towel. Next we put out the centerpiece. Now, I don't care where you go to church, who you voted for, or how much money you got in your checkin' account or lack thereof, nobody ain't got no kind of reason for not havin' a centerpiece on their table when they got company comin' over to sup at their trailer. It ain't that hard and it don't cost nothin' to make a centerpiece, which I'll show you how to make later in chapter 8. So go ahead and put that centerpiece on the table. Now place the salt and pepper shaker on one side of that and the ketchup on the opposite side. Then put the Miracle Whip on one of the empty sides and the mustard on the remainin' side. The last thing you put out is the place mats. Once you've finished puttin' them out, you've successfully prepared your table.

Where to put the plates and plastic utensils is also rather simple. The paper plate is set right in the middle of the place mat. Next you'll place the more expensive plastic/Styrofoam plate on top of this. Now if for some reason you're out of these foam plates, then go ahead and substitute two or three additional paper plates on top of the one that already rests on the place mat. Just remember that if you do substitute, then you'll need to put a few grains of salt between the one that's already on the table and the ones you place on top of it. This will make it easier for your guests to pick up the substituted plates without cartin' the single one off with 'em when they go to the buffet line. If y'all are startin' off with a salad first, then the plastic bowl should go right dab on top of all them plates you got on the place mat.

The rule of thumb for dinner utensils is that you eat in or start with the forks, spoons, and knives that are farthest from the plate and end your meal with the ones that are right next to the plate. But since most folks tend to forget which is what, we just make it real simple as you can see in the illustration below.

As you notice, the plastic salad fork that you melted the handles down on so it looks different from your regular dinner fork and the plastic spoon are placed right above the plates and salad bowl. To the left is the plastic dinner fork and to the right is the plastic knife. If you're

servin' a special dessert, wait till you set it out to pass out the plastic sporks that you got from your favorite fast-food restaurant. Also, hold off on puttin' out the stir straws or sticks until you serve the after-dinner coffee.

The tea or soda pop convenience store cup should go just to the upper right of the place mat. Now you'll notice that I've included a much smaller cup just to the right of the tea or soda pop cup. Personally you won't find that cup if you come to my trailer for dinner on account of the fact that I don't allow dippin' durin' meals, but let me clear this up right here and now that not puttin' out a spit cup on the table is clearly by my personal choice only. Protocol calls for a spit cup at each settin', but that is one element that I don't encourage and have personally removed from dinners when I entertain. And if no one smokes at your table, then the ashtray at the upper left of the place mat can be removed as well.

Once the place mat and all the items are placed on the table, I add the last two items, the napkin and the place card. I like to do somethin' special for all my guests when they come over to eat. I have found that even though I am only usin' paper towels or McDonald's napkins, I still like my guests to feel like I've gone all out for them, so I also use napkin holders. My homemade napkin holders are very easy to make. Simply follow the steps below and then when you're done, place the napkin with the holder around it just to the left of the plastic dinner fork.

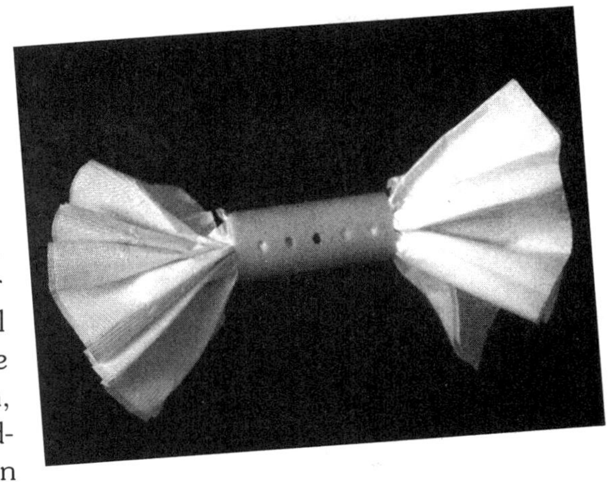

**Supplies**

Can of spray-on adhesive glue
4 hair curlers
Assorted tubes of glitter, your favorite color

**1.** Apply a generous coatin' of spray-on adhesive glue to a hair curler.

**2.** Sprinkle it with glitter, then set it aside to dry.

**3.** Shake the curler over a trash can to get all the loose glitter off.

**4.** Take your napkin and stick one end through the curler. Grab that end and pull the napkin through until it is equally proportioned on both ends.

As you will see in the next part of this chapter, the seatin' arrangement is very important at a dinner, which is why you're gonna need some kind of place cards. There are many ways of makin' a fun place card, but I found that the ones my sister gave me for Christmas one year are not only festive and enjoyable, but they also seem to be the topic of conversation when people see 'em settin' out on the dinner table. Accordin' to Donna Sue, they're really easy to make, and as you'll soon see, she was right. Why, in no time you're gonna have four place cards

that are sure to make your dinners the talk of the trailer park.

**SUPPLIES**

4 mousetraps
Piece of newspaper
Can of spray-on adhesive
Tube of clear, silver, opaque, or white glitter
4- x 3-inch piece of cardboard
Scissors
Hot glue gun
Hot glue stick
Regular sheet of yellow construction paper
Pen or marker
Two-sided tape

**1.** Take four mousetraps new or used and give 'em a good cleanin' with soap and water. Set 'em aside to dry thoroughly overnight.

**2.** Set the traps on a piece of newspaper and give them a coatin' of spray-on adhesive.

**3.** Sprinkle a little bit of clear, silver, opaque, or white glitter on the traps. Let dry.

**4.** Over a trash can, shake all the loose glitter off the traps.

**5.** Take a piece of cardboard and cut out four 3 x 1-inch rectangles.

**6.** Hot-glue a rectangle onto the part of a mousetrap where you'd normally place the cheese. Do this to all four traps.

**7.** Cut the yellow construction paper into four 3 x 1-inch rectangles.

**8.** Write each of your guests' names on one of the rectangles.

**9.** Put a piece of two-sided tape on the back of each paper and press it to the cardboard on the trap.

**10.** Place each trap at the top of the place mat.

A nice thing about these place cards is that they can serve three functions: they tell your guests where to sit, they make a great ice breaker for new guests, and, if needed, they can be used as mousetraps after dinner. I know that might sound horrid, but if you think of it this way, when that poor mouse finally does meet its end and goes on to collect its heavenly reward, covered with all that glitter, it'll at least be thinkin' it died in some fancy discothèque.

## Who Sets Where

When it comes to layin' out your seatin' plan, there're only four things to remember:

**1.** The host and hostess set opposite from each other at the ends of the table.
**2.** Never separate any couple that's been married for less than a year or are engaged (you can seat 'em across from each other if you like).
**3.** All the men set at one end and the women at the other (this assures that nobody gets upset 'cause somebody else was tryin' to pick up somebody else's spouse at the table, which is stupid anyway, 'cause who cares about sex when there's food on your plate).
**4.** And always put the people you like to talk to the most as close to you as possible.

## Dinnertime

Guests can easily be brought from the livin' room to the dinner table by simply announcin' that it is time to eat. You can do this by usin' one of these popular trailer park sayin's.

**1.** All right, get your butts up and get in here.
**2.** OK, folks, this stuff ain't gonna eat itself.
**3.** Last one to the table has to kiss me.
**4.** I've worked on this dinner all day long, so whenever you want to come in here and give it a try, come on ahead.
**5.** Come on, let's go.
**6.** You better hurry up and get in here before I eat all the beans.
**7.** It's ready.
**8.** I hope y'all ain't too hungry 'cause I've already started.
**9.** Is that Vance Pool I see walkin' up our driveway?
**10.** Dew, did you break wind again in the livin' room?

## The Blessin'

Grace should always be said at the dinner table when company is in the house. After all, you don't want 'em to think you're heathens or nothin'. In the past it was thought that you should invite one of your guests to say the blessin', which is a tradition that I used to follow. But after havin' Sister Bertha over and havin' to reheat everything back up after she got done sayin' the dinner prayer, I've now found it easier to just do it myself. So I suggest that regardless of how bashful or shy you might be, unless you feel like eatin' a piece of microwaved chicken and cold biscuits, that you say grace. It doesn't have to be some long-drawn-out thing. After all, your guests didn't come to your trailer for a prayer vigil. So keep it sweet and simple. Just make sure you thank the good Lord for the good food, the good friends, and a win for the Razorbacks. I asked Pastor Ida May Bee and she has assured me that there's absolutely nothin' wrong with addin' the phrase "Go Pigs," into a prayer.

## How to Serve the Meal

More and more lately I'm seein' at trailer park dinners that the host or hostess is actually servin' the food. In these events, they'll set everything on the table to be passed around by the guests, but if you need somethin' like a refill on sugar tea or another plate 'cause yours melted or you poked a hole in it, then it's the hostess that will get up and take care of your needs. Now I will go over this kind of meal servin' but personally I prefer the traditional way of servin' guests, buffet style. After all, just 'cause I'm hostessin' don't mean that I don't want to enjoy my meal as well. Sure, I'll be glad to tell you where the extra napkins are or where I keep my mop when you knock over your drink, but just don't expect me to get up from the table unless it's to get another helpin'. So I say hold on to tradition by parkin' your butt in your assigned chair if you're the hostess, and let your guests fend for themselves. After all, you did all the cookin' didn't you?

If you're at one of them dinners where they pass the food items around, you needn't worry, 'cause I'm gonna tell you how it's done. As soon as grace has been said, and the amens uttered, you're to pick up whatever dish is in front of you and pass it directly to your left, after you've helped yourself to a good-size helpin' of course. Just remember that in this case, right is wrong, and you'll do just fine. And if you're busy helpin' yourself to, say, the corn, and somethin' you don't like, say, beets, comes to you in the process, simply turn to the person on the left of you and tell 'em that you don't "eat that crap." Make sure you point towards the beets with your head, and then ask 'em if they'll get 'em out of your way. This lets the person with the beets know that they're to skip you, while at the same time it gives the person whose waitin' for the corn the green light to reach over you and accept the beets from the other diner. But say you love beets, and are still workin' that dang corn, then simply instruct that person to just set 'em down and you'll get to 'em. That or ask 'em to put a good-size servin' on your plate for you.

When servin' buffet style, just get everyone around the table by where their place cards are—they ain't got to sit down for this part—say grace, and point 'em over to the area of the counter where you got the salad and dressin's all set out. They can continue to talk amongst themselves as they dive in. Just make sure that you got the rest of the meal covered with foil so nobody gets ahead of your game plan and munches down on that. You made the dang salad, so everybody is gonna eat the dang salad! When you've finished your salad, go ahead and uncover the next items to be eaten. Leave the salad out though, just in case someone wants seconds. Usually trailer folk don't go back for seconds on regular old lettuce salads, but it's a nice thought anyways.

## The Menu

You can serve anything you want, but I'd stay away from fish or seafood unless you know for sure that your guests eat that kind of stuff. Personally I think you can never go wrong with a good casserole (check out chapter 5 for some of my favorite casserole recipes) and some side dishes. And you got to have bread of some kind. Now I say that only to be reminded of the time some fool gave me a roll with a piece of fruit in it. There's nothin' really wrong with fruity bread, and I know it has its place in a meal, but not at dinnertime and not with my meal. So save that fruit bread for breakfast unless you got a sugar sauce to pour over it.

## When to Crumb the Table

The "crumbin' of the table" is so often done at the wrong time at most dinners that it almost breaks my heart. It really is very easy and shouldn't be the bother that it is in today's world. Just remember that right after you've finished dinner and have sat back down with your dessert, you should crumb your dinin' area. All you got to do is take the back side of your arm and, in one quick smooth move, brush the crumbs off from the table where you've been eatin' onto the floor. Then simply brush your arm off before continuin'. It's easy enough for anyone to do and is a sign to your guests that you're ready for dessert.

## When to Serve Dessert and Coffee

After you've finished your dinner, and not a minute before, you can go ahead and serve the dessert and coffee. Now I just let folks help themselves to the dessert, which I always keep up on the kitchen counter, unless of course I've made somethin' real fancy-like that needs a special presentation.

## When to Clear Off the Table

This part is real easy. What I do is while my husband and guests are helpin' themselves to the sweets, I go ahead and pull the trash can right up to the table and toss everything off into the trash. After I put the trash can back where it goes, I pull out the coffee cups, stir straws or sticks, creamer, sugar, and the sporks and put 'em on the table. This way when my guests sit down everything but the coffee is right there for 'em. While I get the coffee pot, it gives 'em a chance to crumb the table. After servin' coffee, I'll help myself to the dessert and rejoin the table.

## Who Shuffles First?

When you're invited over to dinner in a trailer park, it usually means that games will follow after you've finished your dessert. Sometimes those games will be simple, fun-to-play board games, but for the most part the game ends up bein' cards. Yes, every person worth their weight in propane knows how to play hearts, spades, continental or Michigan rummy, and canasta. And what would trailer life be without a mean cutthroat night of Uno, Skip-Bo, or Wahoo. We sure do love our card games. So once you've finished with your dessert, take your plate and throw it in the trash can, fill up your drink, pull out your bifocals, and get ready for a game that's played with as much cunnin', skill, and strategy as any battlefield ever saw.

After the table's been cleared of all the extra stuff that ain't needed for cards, the decks are brought out, the game is named, and every person at the table draws a card. The person who wins the draw will be the first one to be dealt to, meanin' that the individual on the winner's right starts off the game of fun and passion by dealin' first.

When it comes to cards in a trailer home there are three things to remember. If a person don't want to play cards, don't make 'em 'cause they'll most likely mess the whole thing up. After all, there's a reason they don't want to play, and that reason might just be 'cause they're bad, and if I get stuck with 'em as a partner, somebody's gonna pay for makin' 'em join in. Second, there ain't ever a reason to cheat. If I catch you cheatin', I won't say nothin' to your face. As a matter of fact, I'll just keep playin' like I didn't see nothin' and then the next day I'll bring you over a big old hot batch of my famous Ex-Lax chip cookies. And of course as long as there's breath in my lungs and blood runnin' through my veins, you'll never eat casserole in my trailer again. And last but not least, number three is simply: Remember, folks, it's just a party game.

## We've Enjoyed Your Company, Now Get the Heck Out

It's a safe bet to try to leave by the time the clock strikes 9:30 P.M. If you're in the middle of a game, make sure you, the guest, let everyone know that you've got to head out when the game is finished. If your host replies back with a regret that you've got to go after the game, don't take that as a reason to stay later. The host is more than likely just bein' nice. After the game, if you thank the host for havin' you and he still says that he wishes you could stay, then he means it. Stick around for another game if you can. At the end of that game, go home no matter what the host says.

If you got a guest that won't leave regardless of how many hints you've dropped, simply open the front door and say, "I smell smoke. Oh my gosh, is that your car on fire?" When the guest goes out to check it, close the door and lock it. Enough said.

## Leftovers

If you got leftovers that you know you and your spouse won't finish, give some of 'em to your guests to take home. Now, although this has never been a problem for me personally, I still know what to do if it should happen. Put the guest's helpin's in some of your trailer park Tupperware (empty Cool Whip bowls, butter tubs, peanut butter containers, or other reusable containers) and tell 'em to keep an' enjoy. Make sure you also instruct 'em to keep the containers. I personally like to do all this before we play cards so that I can put their leftovers in the freezer; and that way if they got a long way to travel, say, across town, it will stay good regardless of the outside temperature.

If there are any tricks or questions that I haven't covered concernin' dinner parties, please feel free to contact me vial e-mail at *rubylot18@aol.com* or come to my Web page at *www.rubyannboxcar.com* and post your question in my guest book.

## Ask Ruby Ann . . .

Dear Ruby Ann,

My question is real simple. I'm just wondering if it's all right to serve finger bowls before and after dinner?

Shanna
Toronto, Canada

Dear Shanna,

Finger bowls are kind of a touchy subject with me on account of how deceivin' they can be to guests. It just seems like when folks see 'em for the first time, they don't know if they should drink the stuff or what. I remember one time I'd been forced to serve small bowls of chicken broth on account of the fact that I'd wrongfully thought I had more cans of broth in the cupboard than I actually did. Well, one of my guest who was very posh and well-to-do took this small portion of warm chicken broth for a finger bowl and began dippin' his fingers in it. Not wantin' to be thought of as folks with bad social habits, all my guests unknowingly followed this fella's lead. Needless to say, I just removed the bowls as soon as I saw what was takin' place and kept quiet about the whole thing. Of course after him and my other guests left, me and my husband nearly cracked a rib from laughin'. Because of this, I've just left finger bowls out of my dinner parties all together.

Instead, I let all the guests know that we got a fresh bar of Lava in the bathroom, and at the end of the meal I pass out them hand wipes that me and my husband, Dew, always pocket by the handfuls when we go to casinos to gamble. Even if I'm only playin' black jack or three card poker, I still make my way over to the slot machines to gather up a good helpin' of those. After all, I helped pay for them little packaged hand wipes as well as the west tower in most of them joints.

Love, Kisses, and Trailer Park Wishes,
Ruby Ann Boxcar

# Chapter 5

# Cookin' in a Quick

*The black ribbon, which was introduced in our area just ten years ago at both the state and county fairs, serves as an award of achievement as well as a much needed warnin' to those in attendance. Needless to say, my Me-Ma, who now resides at the Last Stop Nursing Home has won a black ribbon in each cookin' category for the past ten years straight. Please remember to keep her and the fair judges from eleven years ago in your prayers.*

By now y'all have gotten the idea that trailer park food is good, simple, easy-to-make dishes that contain most things y'all would have around your kitchen. And I know from the many e-mails and letters that I get from all my fans and friends that y'all have come to make many of these dishes regular meals, which, now that y'all know how to eat good, is why I've decided to move on to this book. But with that all said, there are still a few areas regardin' food in a trailer park that we never had the chance to touch on in my last three books. One of these areas would be last-minute cookin'. For example, let's say your husband walks in and informs you that after runnin' into Pastor Ida May Bee and her husband, Brother Woody Bee, while gettin' the mail, he invited 'em to join y'all for supper in an hour and a half. Well, wouldn't you know it, you ain't been to the Piggly Wiggly or the Winn Dixie yet this week and now with this announcement you got to figure out a way to feed a good home-cooked meal to at least four people (who knows who else will stop by), and the clock is tickin'. You got a problem all right, but don't panic. I know sometimes it looks hopeless, but don't worry, 'cause I got the answer with just one little word . . . casserole. That's right, we trailer park cooks have found this simple yet fulfillin' dish just the ticket for last-minute eatin' guests. And since you can literally mix just about anything together and throw it in a casserole dish, you ain't got to go ballistic searchin' your fridge and cabinets for ingredients. Mind you, you'll still want to think about taste when you create that quick casserole.

Lord knows I'll never forget the time Me-Ma had some of us over to her trailer for a special event back when she used to occupy Lot #16. I can honestly say that I don't recall what we were all there for, but I'll never forget that a raisin liver pickle casserole topped with an apricot jam cottage cheese glaze don't go down easy, even with ketchup. Needless to say, we put her in the home soon after and threw that casserole dish in the trash 'cause we couldn't get the smell out.

So once you've read your husband the riot act and told him for the umpteenth time to never invite anybody includin' Elvis impersonators over for any meal of the day without talkin' to you first, you can get ready to put that casserole together. Now, if you're like me and most other socialites in the trailer park, you will be even less stressed out by this last-minute cookin' job on account of the fact that you've already got one or two different casseroles tightly wrapped and stored up in your freezer. Since these dishes tend to last a good long time frozen, we always make sure to have at least one on hand, unless of course the paychecks have been a little thin and we've had to cut corners on our budget with a chain saw. But since casseroles can be made pretty cheap, typically we'll have one cold and ready to go. Of course, there are a few things you should always remember when you're preparin' one of these main course dishes with the sole intention of freezin' it.

**1.** Never overcook: Simply let the ingredients finish cookin' while you reheat the casserole in the oven.

**2.** Put your prepared casserole in a big plastic container that can easily be stored in the freezer. When you're ready to cook, just dump it back into a casserole dish and put in the oven. As it warms up you can carefully spread it out into the pan little by little.

**3.** Always undersalt and underseason the casserole, since freezin' tends to make the taste of some seasonin's, like cloves, pepper, and garlic, much stronger and others, such as salt, onion, and sage, get bland.

**4.** Never freeze casseroles with egg whites in it 'cause they end up tastin' like bits of rubber. You can always boil an egg, chop it up and stir it in or sprinkle it over the top of your casserole after you've heated it in the oven.

**5.** Pasta shells get all soft and soggy when you reheat 'em, so stay away from freezin' any casseroles that got noodles in 'em.

Now, on the followin' pages you're gonna find some of our most favorite casserole dishes at the High Chaparral Trailer Park. None of these have been featured in any of my cookbooks or on my Web pages, which means you ain't got these yet, at least not from me. Some of 'em can be frozen, while others can't, but if you follow the five steps that I've just given you, y'all will be able to tell which ones are which. And since all of these dishes make up your meal, you ain't got to serve anythin' else other than maybe some bread (store-bought is just fine), a beverage (Dr Pepper, RC Cola, or sweet tea will work great), and an easy dessert (a couple of scoops of ice cream topped with a cookie you've crushed). And since these only take about 45 minutes to bake, you got plenty of time to make yourself presentable as well.

## Little Linda's Pork Chop Casserole

*With food like this, you know why the tables at the Blue Whale Strip Club are steel reinforced.*

Makes 6 servin's

6 pork chops
⅓ cup flour
½ teaspoon salt
¼ teaspoon paprika
4 tablespoons finely chopped onion
4 tablespoons ketchup
⅓ cup boilin' water
1 cup cooked brown rice

Roll the pork chops in the flour, place 'em in a casserole dish, sprinkle with salt and paprika, add everythin' else but the rice, cover with foil, and bake for 45 minutes at 350 degrees F. Uncover and add the rice. Recover and cook for 15 more minutes.

—LITTLE LINDA, LOT #20

## Connie Kay's Pizza Party Casserole

*I can't begin to tell y'all how many times I've bought unneeded Mary Kay or Avon products from her just so I could attend one of her gatherin's when she was servin' this dish.*

Makes around 4 servin's

1 pound ground beef
½ teaspoon onion salt
½ teaspoon garlic salt
1 teaspoon oregano
½ teaspoon salt
1 regular can condensed tomato soup
⅓ cup water
2 cups cooked wide noodles
1 cup shredded cheese (prepackaged pizza cheese is best, but any will do)

Place your first five ingredients in a skillet and cook until the meat is brown. Drain and put in a casserole dish with your next three ingredients. Add the cheese, cover, and bake for 20 minutes at 350 degrees F. Uncover and bake for an additional 10 minutes.

—Connie Kay, Lot #13

## Lorena Bobbit Casserole

*This casserole is a cut above the rest.*

Makes 6 servin's

1 pound wienies
1 large onion, diced
½ regular package egg noodles
1 regular can tomato soup
¼ pound Velveeta cheese, cubed

Take a knife and cut up the wienies. Throw 'em into a skillet with the onion and brown over medium heat.

Follow the directions on the package and boil your noodles. Drain 'em. Mix everything together in a casserole dish and bake at 350 degrees F. for 1 hour.

—TINA FAYE STOPENBLOTTER, LOT #17

## The Official Sweat Scarves of Elvis Fan Club Casserole

*I can't begin to tell y'all how many times me and the rest of the gals have cried over a plate of this stuff while we set around and listened to the King's records.*

Serves 6

2 cups leftover fried chicken, cut up and deboned
1 regular can mushroom soup
1 regular can chicken noodle soup
1 small can evaporated milk
1 to 1½ cups crushed cornflakes
Salt

Mix the first four items together in a casserole dish. Top with the cornflakes and salt. Bake for 35 to 40 minutes at 350 degrees F.

—RUBY ANN BOXCAR, LOT #18

## Trailer Park Pot Pie Casserole

*This dish is so good, even when one of my sister's one-night stands has sobered up, he'll still stick around until lunchtime if he smells this in the oven.*

Makes 4 servin's

2 tablespoons flour
1½ tablespoons margarine
1 cup chicken broth
¼ cup milk
¼ teaspoon salt
⅛ teaspoon pepper
1½ cups cooked chicken
½ cup cooked rice
1 package pop-open refrigerator biscuits

Blend the flour and margarine together. Slowly add the broth and the milk. Cook on medium in a pan until it thickens, stirrin' the entire time. Take off the heat and add the salt, pepper, and chicken. Put the rice in a casserole dish and then pour on this sauce. Put the biscuits on top of this and cover with foil. Let it bake at 400 degrees F. for 15 minutes. Uncover and cook for an additional 10 or 15 minutes.

—Donna Sue Boxcar, Lot #6

## Wendy Bottom's Cow in the Garden Casserole

*This actually tastes a lot better than it sounds.*

Makes 5 servin's

1 pound ground beef
1 small onion, chopped
1 green bell pepper, chopped
1 regular can string beans, drained
1 regular can undiluted tomato soup
2 cups mashed potatoes
½ teaspoon salt
⅛ teaspoon pepper
1 egg

Brown the ground beef along with the onion and pepper in a skillet. Add the string beans and tomato soup and mix. Put this mixture in a casserole dish and let it bake for 30 minutes uncovered at 350 degrees F.

Mix together the potatoes, salt, pepper, and egg. Put this on top of the casserole and bake for another 15 to 20 minutes.

—Wendy Bottom, Lot #4

## Opal Lamb-Inman's No-Meat Bake

*Your guests won't care that you ain't servin' no kind of meat in this dish.*

Makes 4 servin's

1 10-ounce can spinach, rinsed and chopped
2 tablespoons margarine
1 small onion, chopped
2 tablespoons flour
Salt to taste
Pinch pepper
2 cups plain yogurt
2 cups Cheddar cheese, grated

Put your spinach in a skillet, cover, and steam with the water that is still on the leaves from the rinsin'. Let it steam until it wilts. Put it in a bowl and set aside.

Melt your margarine in the same skillet and then add your onion. Cook until the onion is soft. Add the flour and stir over a medium heat for a moment. Add your salt and pepper, and then gradually add the yogurt, whiskin' it in small amounts. Once you've added all the yogurt, add the spinach, and mix until the spinach gets a nice coat of the yogurt mixture. Take off the heat and add the cheese. Pour it all into a greased 8- x 4-inch pan. Let it bake for around 20 minutes at 350 degrees F. Serve hot and enjoy!

—Opal Lamb-inman, Lot #1

## The Taco Tackle Shack's Monday Special

*This wonderful casserole don't last till Tuesday, I can tell you.*

Makes 6 servin's

1 pound ground beef
½ cup chopped onions
¼ cup diced celery
1 teaspoon salt
¼ teaspoon pepper
1 pound canned chili
1 cup corn chips
1 cup diced Velveeta cheese

Brown the meat and then add the onion and celery, cookin' until the veggies get tender. Add the salt and pepper. Add the chili and stir. Put a layer of the chips in a greased casserole dish followed by the chili mixture, then some cheese. Repeat. Bake in the oven at 350 degrees F. for 10 to 12 minutes.

—Lois Bunch, Lot #3

## Cheeseburger and Fries Casserole

*Kitty says Kyle loves to drink a cold beer with this.*
*Shock surprise!*

Makes 6 servin's

2 pounds of ground beef, browned and drained
1 regular can cream of mushroom soup
1 regular can cheddar cheese soup
½ soup can of water
20-ounce bag frozen fries

Mix the ground beef, both soups, and the water all together in a bowl. Grease up a casserole dish and dump the mixture in it. Cover this with the fries. Cook for 50 to 60 minutes at 350 degrees F. Eat hot with ketchup.

—Kitty Chitwood, Lot #11

# Give Me That Old-Time Religion Casserole

*I don't know if this dish is sanctified, but it sure is good!*

Makes 6 servin's

2 pounds cooked sweet potatoes
½ cup pecans, chopped
1 cup cooked and cubed ham
1½ cups pineapple juice
¼ cup sugar
¼ cup brown sugar
1 tablespoon cornstarch
2 tablespoons margarine

Put the sweet potatoes, pecans, and ham into a casserole dish. Set aside. Mix the pineapple juice, sugars, cornstarch, and margarine together. Pour over the potato mixture in the casserole dish. Bake an hour, bastin' often, at 300 degrees F.

—SISTER BERTHA, LOT #12

# Lulu Bell's Hungry Simple Gal Corn Casserole

*This ain't bad for a grown woman who still leaves out cookies and milk every year for Santa. Thank goodness I got a key to her trailer and she's a heavy sleeper.*

Makes 8 servin's

6 slices crisp bacon, broken into bits
1 cup milk
2 regular cans corn
3 hot dog buns, torn into small pieces
¾ teaspoon salt
½ teaspoon chili powder
1 cup shredded Velveeta cheese
1 (4-ounce) can sliced mushrooms

Mix it all together and put in a casserole dish to bake uncovered at 350 degrees F. for 50 minutes.

—LULU BELL BOXCAR, LOT #8

## Faye Faye LaRue's Tuna Treat Casserole

*Now, I ain't big on tuna, so I really can't tell you if this is good or not, but I do know that she makes this dish so often that durin' the summer months her trailer smells like this casserole.*

Makes 6 servin's

⅓ cup milk
1 regular can cream of mushroom soup
1 regular package of frozen peas, cooked without salt
1 (7-ounce) can tuna fish, drained
4 eggs, separated
¼ cup tiny cubes Velveeta cheese

Preheat your oven to 400 degrees F.

Mix the milk and soup in a casserole dish, then add the drained peas. Mix well. Add the tuna and toss until mixed. Bake uncovered for 12 minutes.

Beat your yolks until they get to a lemon color. Next beat the whites till they stand in peaks. Carefully fold these two together and put on top of the cheese. Bake for 20 more minutes.

—FAYE FAYE LARUE, LOT #17

## Tater Doggies

*I guess this dish answers all the questions of who the real cook is over in Lot #19.*

Makes 8 servin's

6 wienies, diced
4 potatoes, cooked and diced
2 tablespoons minced onion
¼ cup margarine, soft
1 cup peas, cooked
1 teaspoon mustard
1 cup cream mushroom soup
¼ teaspoon salt
¼ teaspoon pepper

Mix the wienies, potatoes, onions, and margarine together in a casserole. Mix in the rest. Bake for 25 minutes at 350 degrees F.

—HARRY LOMBARDI, LOT #19

# Ollie White's Bologna Bake

*God bless her, Ollie don't get lots of unexpected visitors much lately, and I ain't sure why.*

Makes 4 servin's

3 cups cooked noodles
1 cup chopped bologna
½ teaspoon salt
⅛ teaspoon pepper
1 cup milk
½ cup crackers, crushed
1 teaspoon margarine

Take a greased casserole dish and put in a layer of noodles. Now add a layer of bologna. Repeat. Top with salt, pepper, and milk. Sprinkle on the crackers and dot with the margarine. Bake at 400 degrees F. for 30 minutes.

—Ollie White, Lot #10

# Snap, Crackle, Pop Me Casserole

*Kenny and Donny have the cutest little black leather casserole dish carrier that they always use when they bring this to any covered-dish function.*

Makes 8 servin's

1 pound ground beef
1 onion, chopped
½ box Rice Krispies
2 regular cans chicken and rice soup
1 regular can cream of chicken soup

Brown your ground beef and onion together in a pan. Drain and mix it with all the rest of the ingredients in the casserole dish. Bake for 45 to 50 minutes at 375 degrees F.

—Kenny Lynn, Lot #15

# Mother Father Tuna Casserole

*Juanita says that she got this from her second cousin, Danica, who works as a hair stylist at a prison in Colorado.*

Makes 6 servin's

1 regular bag any kind of pasta
1 regular can cream of mushroom soup
2 regular cans tuna
1 cup shredded Cheddar cheese
1 cup shredded mozzarella cheese
1 regular can mushroom stems and pieces

Boil the pasta, drain, and then mix everything together in a casserole dish. Bake at 350 degrees F. for 50 minutes. Turn up to broil for 2 to 5 minutes to make it a bit crunchier.

—JUANITA HIX, LOT #9

Now, I got to include this one last casserole recipe even though it is more of a side dish/dessert casserole. If you have any of this left over, pour the juice off into a separate bowl and put it in the freezer to use as a syrup over ice cream or even a drizzle for a simple pound cake.

# Donna Sue's Drunken Tater Magic Casserole

*Trust me when I tell y'all that you're gonna want to have some pillows and blankets handy 'cause after a few helpin's of this dish folks are gonna want to lie down.*

Makes 6 servin's

5 pounds canned and cooked yams
1 (1-pound) box brown sugar
1 stick margarine
1 tablespoon molasses
1¾ cups Kahlúa
1 tablespoon salt
1 teaspoon cinnamon
1 bag miniature marshmallows

Place the yams in large casserole dish and sprinkle the entire box of brown sugar over them to completely cover them. Cut the stick of margarine into small pieces and sprinkle those over the brown sugar. Drizzle the molasses mixed with 1 cup of the Kahlúa over the entire mixture and finish off by dustin' lightly with the salt and cinnamon.

Place in 350 degree F. oven for 30 to 45 minutes until bubbly. Top with the rest of the Kahlúa and the marshmallows and cook an additional 3 to 5 minutes until they develop a light brown edge.

—DONNA SUE BOXCAR, LOT #6

## Ask Ruby Ann . . .

Dear Ruby Ann,

What is the difference between "white trash" cooking and the kind of cooking that you and your neighbors do?

T.T.
Shreveport, LA

Dear T.T.,

Thanks for that wonderful question. Lots of people like yourself who just don't know that there's a difference between white trash and trailer trash are constantly askin' me for "road kill" recipes or how to cook up a possum. But sayin' that white trash and trailer trash, if you will, are similar is like sayin' that puddin' and pie fillin' are one and the same. The answer to your question, T.T., is that white trash go out and kill somethin' or find somethin' dead on the road, bring it home, clean it, and cook it. Trailer trash don't clean nothin'. You should see my bathroom! No, honestly the difference is that trailer folks have the money to buy their groceries at top-of-the-line grocery stores. The only time we ever eat anything that we've personally killed is when we cook up freshly caught fish. Of course my kitchen has never had fish cooked in it since I don't like it, and my husband is one of them fishermen who releases everything he catches. Of course, I tell everybody that the only reason he didn't throw me back was 'cause he couldn't lift me up out of the boat. He comes back with the true reason was 'cause he'd used up all his strength tryin' to get my butt in that boat in the first place. I don't find that very funny and have told him so on several occasions.

Love, Kisses, and Trailer Park Wishes,
Ruby Ann Boxcar

# Chapter 6

# Somewhere It's Cocktail Time

*My fifty-seven-year-old stripper sister, Donna Sue, of Lot #6 has just got a brand-new dog. She's named him Coaster.*

One of my older sister Donna Sue's sayin's is, "Heck, it's five P.M. somewhere in the world!" And of course she's right about that, so she follows that statement with a shot or a guzzle of some kind of alcoholic beverage. That's why when it comes to liquor, my sister and author of *Donna Sue's Down Home Trailer Park Bartendin' Guide,* is the expert in the Boxcar clan as well as the High Chaparral Trailer Park.

Speakin' of drinkin', there are a few others at the High Chaparral Trailer Park who tie for second, right behind my sister Donna Sue, when it comes to bein' experts on booze. My mother in-law, Momma Ballzak, as y'all well know, wouldn't flunk out of a Hooch 101 class, that's for sure. With as much as she puts away, I swear, a snake could come up and bite her, and the doggone thing would pickle instantly. God bless her, she can't hear the TV half the time, but she can hear a can of beer bein' opened a mile way. And my sister's archrival, Faye Faye LaRue, is another one that could build a glass-bottom cruise ship with a year's supply of her empty liquor containers. That gal does to a bottle of booze what dog ugly Opal Lamb-Inman does to a mirror. Just a close-passin' hello from her would leave you tipsy. I kid you not. But if the truth be told, with the recent arrival to the High Chaparral Trailer Park of my sister's good friend and fellow coworker down at the Blue Whale Strip Club, the real tie breaker among my neighbors would have to be the new occupant of Lot #20, Little Linda. You'd expect a gal who tips the scale at around 350 pounds to be able to drink a lot, but Little Linda packs it away like a camel packs away water. She and my sister are the only two people that I've ever known to go into a bar and order by the bottle rather than by the drink. These two would have brought Carrie A. Nation to tears, if you know what I mean. Why, I'll never forget the time a few years back that all three of us went to Las Vegas together.

We stayed at the lovely Westward Ho Hotel and Casino on account of the fact that with all three of us together, most the other hotels wouldn't guarantee our safety on the elevators. The two first-floor rooms that the hotel had available and stuck our big behinds in were very nice, and all in all we had a great stay. Of course I'm sure the casino lost money durin' our two-night vacation on account of all the hot dogs us gals managed to put away. They had this gigantic ¾-pound wienie that I know must have measured around 18 inches in length and 2 or 3 inches around, which they called the Mega-Dog. Folks, I swear I ain't never seen nothin' that big in all my life. But both Donna Sue and Little Linda said they'd seen things that big before. It seems that once a year for their Independence Day shows at the Blue Whale Strip Club Chef Bernie has a big ol' wienie like they serve in Vegas that he adds to the menu for that day's blue plate special. But while Chef Bernie D. Toast charges $2 for his wienie, which is a great price for that much meat, the fine folks at the Westward Ho only rang us up for 75 cents a wienie (I think the price is a little higher nowadays, but still less than two bucks). And at 75 cents, well, you can imagine how many times we packed those things away. Of course I could only eat one per settin', which was also true for Little Linda. And even though my sister ordered two, I only saw her eat one herself. She must have given the second one away or somethin'. She's big hearted like that.

Anyways, we got separated at the Westward Ho on account the fact that I was playin' blackjack at a table and the two tons of terror had decided to find the bar for a little "drinkypoo" as they like to call it. Well, an hour later after I found 'em I asked if they'd been gamblin'. They said that not only had they played the slots, but they had broke even. Bein' a few dollars down, I suggested that we grab a taxi, preferably one of those taxi vans, if our ride to the next casino was to be enjoyable. They agreed, but only after they had a couple of "to-go shots for the road." Since they weren't drivin' I told 'em I'd wait up by the front if they'd hurry up. To my surprise and utter amazement, they came back five minutes later with two of those yard-long funnel cups filled to the top with some kind of liquor. I reminded them that they was only supposed to get shots.

With that they both put those elongated plastic cups to their mouths and began tippin' 'em straight up. Those old drunken cows downed them three-foot containers like they was drinkin' water. After they'd caught their breath and left their new "shot glasses" with the hotel clerk, we grabbed a cab and headed over to the Casino Paris. I really wanted to see that place and would have stayed longer if we hadn't been kicked out 'cause Donna Sue and Little Linda tried to climb the Vegas version of the Eiffel Tower. To this day, and after much repair, if you look real close, you'll notice that the thing still kind of leans to the left. Anyways, we then went over to the Bellagio so I could watch the dancin' water show they put on every thirty minutes. They got these high-pressure jets laid out in their big fountains of water, and after this fog rushes up, they spray out these streams that are choreographed to the music that's playin' at that time. It's supposed to be absolutely gorgeous. Of course when the two drunken heifers that I happened to be with mistook the risin' fog for steam and stripped down to their bra and panties before they both jumped into the pool of water, I kind of knew the only dancin' liquid I'd be seein' that night would be comin' from a drinkin' fountain. Not only were Little Linda and my sister Donna Sue now soakin' wet, but thanks to those high-pressure jets, they were regular.

We went on to other casinos while we were there, where I gambled and they drank. Needless to say, after thirty minutes or less at each stop, we were asked to leave at most of 'em, both on and off the strip. And I kind of got used to bein' embarrassed by my two travelin' companions. But let me say here and now that to be honest, I was in no way embarrassed when the gondola we was on at the Venetian sank to the bottom of the canal shortly after pushin' off. After all, they should have posted signs with the weight restrictions clearly printed on 'em, just like they got in their elevators.

When it came to gamblin', I was the loser out of the three of us. Accordin' to both Little Linda and Donna Sue, they'd done as much gamblin' as they had drinkin', which I doubted. It wasn't until we'd gotten to the airport and were waitin' for our plane to depart that I realized why the two of them had broke even on this trip. Those stupid old cows had been playin' the change machines all this time. Of course they broke even! I could have kicked their drunken sorry bottoms from Las Vegas back to Pangburn, I was so mad. After all, for two whole days they'd led me to believe that I was the world's biggest loser. Now that I look back on it, I got a feelin' that title rests comfortably on the shoulders of the casinos that served free drinks to Little Linda and Donna Sue durin' our trip.

With all that said, my sister is still the queen of the trailer park cocktail hour. Why, she's personally drunk more cocktails than we can name, to be quite honest with you. Of course, part of that reason is the fact that we're all Baptist, which means we don't drink, at least not in public, that is. So our knowledge on cocktails may extend to one or two drinks that we've either stumbled on or created ourselves out of what we had hidden in the closet. An example of this is the drink that was named after me and mentioned in Donna Sue's book. It's called a Rubypolitan and it came into bein' durin' one of my trips where I was promotin' my first book, *Ruby Ann's Down Home Trailer Park Cookbook.* Some nice fella in the hotel restaurant, who'd seen me on the TV that day, sent a drink over to the table where me and my sister was settin'. The drink turned out to be a Cosmopolitan, which I really liked for the most part. When the waiter came by and asked how my drink was I told him that it was just fine, even though I don't care for the cranberry juice. He went on to tell me that you had to have cranberry juice in it so you got that taste as well as that slightly reddish color. Well, I told him that I could do without the tartness and Donna Sue suggested that I should try addin' half a shot of grenadine to it instead. With that, the waiter grabbed up my Cosmopolitan, took it to the bar, and then a few minutes later returned back with what would best be described as resemblin' Hawaiian Punch in a cocktail glass. Well, after one sip of that, I was in heaven and insisted that the waiter try it as well. After a lot of proddin' and pokin', he finally agreed and was just as thrilled by the taste as I was. Of course my sister loved it, but she'd scream the joys of rubbin' alcohol if you know what I mean. That was how the Rubypolitan was created, and it has now become a classic in most bars around the world. It still surprises me how I can walk in to almost any establishment that serves liquor and have the bartender know that an ounce of vodka, ½ ounce of triple sec, ½ ounce of sweet 'n' sour, and ½ ounce of Grenadine shaken and then poured into a martini glass with a lime wedge makes a Rubypolitan. Of course, when I do run across a bartender that don't know how to make one, by the time I leave, you can bet your bottom dollar he does.

And this brings us to the fact that there are some of y'all who are non-Baptist folks as well as some of y'all who are that like to entertain people who can have a few drinks without goin' straight to hell if someone sees 'em, so I asked my sister to please take the time and share a few more fun cocktail recipes with us. After all, beer ain't the only thing folks drink in trailer parks anymore, especially now that we get the Food Network and all them other spicy channels on our television. Now, Donna Sue tells me that all of these drinks are both fun to make and taste just as good. Of course that comes from a gal who once drank a whole bottle of Hi Karate. But if you happen to find these drinks to your likin', then you're bound to love her bartendin' guide, which is also a perfect gift for all your drinkin' friends as well. So get out the ice and grab the mixer, 'cause it's time for a little taste testin'.

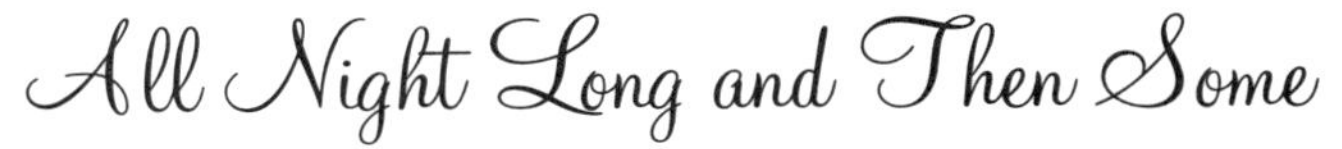


½ ounce Malibu rum
½ ounce Kahlúa
½ ounce vodka
½ ounce dark Creme de Cacao
4 ounces pineapple juice
2 ounces sour mix

Shake all together and then pour into a hurricane glass.

## Apple Crisp

1 ounce Sour Apple Pucker schnapps
½ ounce brandy
1 ounce Baileys Irish Cream
1 scoop vanilla ice cream
¼ cup graham cracker crumbs
1 tablespoon whipped cream for toppin'
pinch cinnamon for toppin'

Pour first five ingredients into blender cup and mix just until smooth. Garnish with whipped cream and cinnamon.

## Arkansas Twister

1 ounce vodka
1 ounce Malibu rum
1 ounce tequila
splash orange juice
splash pineapple juice
splash cream of coconut
1 squirt Grenadine
1 wedge pineapple

Just mix in the shots of rum, vodka, and tequila. Add splashes of the three juices. Top off with Grenadine. Pour in tall glass with ice.

## B-24 Bomber

½ ounce vodka
½ ounce rum
½ ounce tequila
½ ounce gin
½ ounce triple sec
1 ounce orange juice
1 ounce pineapple juice
1 ounce cranberry juice
1 ounce sour mix
1 cup crushed ice

Blend all ingredients in blender until smooth. Pour into a tall glass.

## Banana Boat

1 ounce vodka
1 ounce banana liqueur
1 banana (peel it first)
4 ounces orange juice
2 ounces cream

Pour all ingredients into a blender with a cup of ice and blend until smooth. Serve in a tall glass or brandy snifter.

## Black Gold

4 ounces coffee
¼ ounce triple sec
¼ ounce amaretto
¼ ounce Baileys Irish Cream
¼ ounce hazelnut liqueur
dash cinnamon schnapps
2 tablespoons whipped cream for toppin'

Pour all ingredients except coffee, cinnamon schnapps, and whipped cream into Irish coffee cup, add coffee and schnapps and stir, top with whipped cream.

## Blue Canary

1 ounce gin
1 ounce grapefruit juice
½ ounce Blue Curaçao

Stir all ingredients in a mixin' glass. Strain into a martini glass filled with crushed ice.

## Bottom Bouncer

2 ounces dry gin
3 ounces vodka
4 ounces peach schnapps

Shake and serve in a tall glass with ice.

## Brantini

1½ ounces brandy
1 ounce gin
dash dry vermouth

Shake with ice and strain into a chilled martini glass with ice cubes. Top with a twist of lemon peel.

## Butterball

1 ounce Baileys Irish Cream
½ ounce butterscotch schnapps
8 ounces coffee
2 tablespoons whipped cream for toppin'

Pour into a big hot cup of coffee and top with whipped cream.

## Cafe Boom Boom

½ ounce Frangelico
½ ounce Baileys Irish Cream
¼ ounce brandy
8 ounces coffee
2 tablespoons whipped cream

Pour in tall mug and fill with strong coffee. Top with whipped cream.

## Cherry Fizzer

2 ounces cherry brandy
juice of ½ lemon
splash Grenadine
6 ounces club soda

Put the first three ingredients in a shaker, shake with ice, and strain into a highball glass half filled with ice cubes. Fill with club soda and put a cherry on top.

## Derby Cocktail

¾ ounce peach brandy
2 ounces gin

Shake with ice and strain into a cocktail glass.

## Dixie Whiskey

2 ounces bourbon
½ teaspoon powdered sugar
dash bitters
¼ ounce triple sec
½ ounce white creme de menthe

Shake with ice and strain into a rocks glass.

## Gatherin' Nuts and Berries

1 ounce Frangelico
1 ounce Chambord raspberry liqueur
3 ounces half-and-half

Pour Frangelico and Chambord raspberry liqueur over ice into a 6-ounce glass and fill with cream.

## Grandma's Magic Elixir

2 ounces whiskey
2 ounces prune juice
lemon wedge
lemon slice

Pour into a rocks glass, squeeze the juice from the lemon wedge, serve at room temperature and garnish with a lemon slice.

## Gray Hawaiian

½ ounce gin
½ ounce vodka
½ ounce light rum
½ ounce tequila
½ ounce Blue Curaçao
½ ounce Grenadine
splash pineapple juice
splash sweet and sour mix

Shake all the ingredients, and strain into a chilled cocktail glass.

## Hawaiian Cocktail

2 ounces gin
1 tablespoon pineapple juice
½ ounce triple sec

Shake all the ingredients together and then strain into a cocktail glass filled with shaved ice.

## Help Wanted

1 ounce apricot brandy
1 ounce bourbon whiskey
dash of lemon juice

Shake with ice and strain into a cocktail glass.

## Hot Chocolate Russian

2 ounces Kahlúa
1 ounce vodka
6 ounces hot chocolate

Pour Kahlúa and vodka into a mug and fill with hot chocolate. Stir.

## Hot Cinnamon Apple

1½ ounces cinnamon schnapps
6 ounces hot apple cider
2 tablespoons whipped cream for toppin'
1 cinnamon stick
dash nutmeg

Pour schnapps into a mug. Add hot cider until full. Top with whipped cream and add a cinnamon stick. Dust with nutmeg.

## Irish Mint Kiss

1 ounce Baileys Irish Cream
½ ounce Rumple Minze peppermint schnapps

3 ounces coffee
2 tablespoons whipped cream

Combine ingredients in a mug and top with whipped cream.

## Make Mine a Double Sour

¾ ounce blended whiskey
¾ ounce gin
juice of ½ lemon
½ teaspoon powdered sugar
½ teaspoon Grenadine

Shake with ice and strain into a rocks glass.

## Mexican Coffee

¾ ounce coffee liqueur
¾ ounce amaretto
6 ounces hot coffee
2 tablespoons milk
2 tablespoons sugar
1 tablespoon cinnamon
2 tablespoons whipped cream for toppin'

Mix the cinnamon and sugar together. Dip rim of a mug in milk, then in cinnamon sugar mixture. Pour alcohol into glass and fill with coffee. Add the whipped cream to the top.

## Nuclear Plant Drinkin' Water

1½ ounces melon liqueur
2 ounces pineapple juice
1½ ounces coconut rum

Mix ingredients in a shaker with ice and strain into highball glass. Fill blender to the top with ice cubes. Add remainin' ingredients. Blend until ice is crushed, addin' more until texture is thick like a shake.

## Orange Bullet

1½ ounces gin
1½ ounces orange juice
1 tablespoon lime juice
3 ounces ginger ale

Shake and strain into a cocktail glass. Fill with ginger ale and stir well.

## Pucker Up and Kiss Me, Stupid Martini

1½ ounces gin
1½ ounces Sour Apple Pucker schnapps

Shake with ice and strain into a chilled martini glass.

## Razzel Dazzel 'Em

1 ounce blackberry liqueur
½ ounce creme de cassis
½ ounce coffee liqueur
4 ounces coffee
2 tablespoons whipped cream for toppin'

Pour liqueurs into Irish coffee mug, add coffee, top with whipped cream.

## Red Hot Lovin'

½ ounce bourbon
½ ounce amaretto
½ ounce Southern Comfort
¼ ounce sloe gin
splash triple sec
splash orange juice
splash pineapple juice

Pour all ingredients over ice into a hurricane glass and stir.

½ ounce gin
½ ounce Blue Curaçao
½ ounce Cointreau
½ ounce peach schnapps
½ ounce fruit juice, tropical

Put all in a shaker with ice. Serve in a cold martini glass.

## Sun on the Beach

1 ounce gin
1 ounce Midori melon liqueur
6 ounces orange juice

Combine all the ingredients in a tall glass over ice.

## Tennessee Breeze

2 ounces Jack Daniels
2 ounces pineapple juice
2 ounces orange juice

Pour over ice in a tall glass and stir.

## Tongue Twister

1 ounce brandy
1 ounce Baileys Irish cream
3 ounces cream

Pour into rocks glass with ice and stir.

## Wow Momma

1 ounce gin
½ ounce cherry-flavored brandy
1½ ounces 151-proof rum
1 tablespoon orange juice
1½ teaspoons lime juice

Shake with ice and strain into a chilled martini glass.

Now, folks, let me just take a second to pass on a few words of cocktailin' wisdom that my sister, Donna Sue, told me were very important in regard to booze. The drinks that are listed in this chapter are better known as "specialty cocktails" on account of how they're typically only served on special occasions like birthdays, anniversaries, weddin's, holidays, when special guests come over for cards, Tupperware parties, job promotions, when you find your car or house keys, when you're able to shower without runnin' out of hot water, or you know, other special times. The reason for this is on account of how they take a few minutes to concoct 'em together, whereas your everyday drinks like a vodka soda, scotch and water, or gin and tonic are easy drinks, or as they call 'em in my sister's part of the world, "quickies." So, accordin' to my sister, when you have good friends over for dinner and a few rounds of spades, rummy, or Skip-Bo, make sure you break out the special cocktails if they drink. After all, you're more than likely gonna use the thicker paper plates in their honor, so why not show 'em just how much you enjoy their company by openin' up the bar and icin' down the shaker. Of course, if they don't drink, then just keep the booze under the bed, in the closet, or stashed inside the washin' machine with a small load of your husband's socks and undergarments carefully piled on top the bottles.

Oh, and just 'cause y'all have the bar flowin' with these specialty cocktails, my sister says to keep a few bottles of the standards along with their mixers nearby. Accordin' to her, regardless of how much you love your guests or how special the day might be, you're gonna get tired of havin' to measure out the items called for in these cocktail recipes. Yes, she says that as the night goes on you and your guests are gonna just want to settle for a "quickie" instead. I remember as a little girl, even my daddy was always happy to take one of those, especially after workin' a long hard day. Why, there were even some days when he'd come home durin' lunch and tell momma he was in the mood for a "quickie." She'd pull out the Concord grape wine, take a swig, and send us kids outside to play. Now that I'm an adult, I keep meanin' to ask her what she mixed with that. Most likely it was 7-Up or Sprite.

My sister also says that it is very important to keep lots of ice on hand, 'cause most of these drinks are gonna need ice. Crushed ice is great, as is cubed, but Donna Sue says stay away from the shaved stuff 'cause it melts real fast in your drinks and waters 'em down. But if shaved ice is all you can get your hands on, then shaved ice it is. She personally likes to pack her bags of ice in the bathtub since all the excess water can just run right down the drain, and if you got a few bags stacked up on top of each other, they help to insulate the ice and keep it colder for a longer amount of time. Mind you, even though the bags ain't open, I'd still take a minute or two and clean your tub out first. After all, it just looks better, and if you're like my sister Donna Sue, your tub could really use it.

When it comes to mixers, Donna Sue wants me to remind y'all of a few things. First off, at no time can the words soda or tonic water be substituted with the words glass of water and a package of Alkaseltzer. That just don't cut it, and when your guests start belchin' uncontrollably, they're gonna know that somethin' ain't just right. And red food colorin' and sugar water ain't the same as grenadine regardless of how close they might look in appearance. And as any good God-fearin' person will tell you, Tab ain't got no place in a bar, or in a trailer for that matter. Actually, when it comes to cocktails, Donna Sue assures me that diet-anything should not be used as a mixer, with Diet A & W Root Beer and Diet Sprite or Diet 7-Up bein' the exceptions to the rule. Sorry folks but Diet Dr Pepper is out in cocktail mixin'. However, you can use sugar-free Jell-O when makin' Jell-O shots, which should make you high-protein dieters happy, since you can have vodka and sugar-free Jell-O.

And last but not least accordin' to Donna Sue, make sure that you're always pickin' up empty glasses or offerin' to refresh, refill, or just plain old top off their drinks often as well. This way you can dump any unused garnishes like cherries or such back into their containers rather than waste 'em in a trash can. Obviously if they've been bitten into or such, you can't reuse 'em. You might just leave whatever is left in the bottle and just replenish the liquor and leave out the garnish. Another thing that this practice of gettin' your guests a drink does is help to stop their heavy-handed pourin'.

So just keep these tips in mind, and you and your guests are sure to have a great time—thanks to my drunk of a sister.

## Ask Ruby Ann . . .

Dear Ruby Ann,

My husband, who works at an ad agency, is up for a promotion. His boss is real nice and I think he likes us, but he is often two-faced. I just found out that he and his wife, who I happen to get along with real well, are coming over for dinner tomorrow night. My dilemma is that he likes to have a nice champagne cocktail, but we are on a beer budget and can't afford the good stuff. I have ways of getting the best champagne money can buy, but my husband has forbidden me to use those ways anymore. So I guess my question is simply this, Do you have a recipe that I can use to make a cheap champagne into a delightful champagne cocktail without it tasting like you bought it at the local drugstore?

S. Stephens
Westport, CT

Dear S. Stephens,

I totally understand your situation. Back when my husband had his former boss over to our trailer I tried to do everything I could to impress that man. I even used real Pam instead of the fake stuff in my skillet when I cooked dinner. Well, not only was it a disaster, but my momma kept poppin' in and out of the trailer all night long. I finally just had to lock the doors and threaten her with her life.

Gettin' back to your question, I don't know nothin' about liquor, so I've passed your note on to my sister. Her answer follows.

Love, Kisses, and Trailer Park Wishes,
Ruby Ann Boxcar

Dear S.,

Don't worry, 'cause I got the answer to your question. You know, bein' the sexy entertainer that I am, I always find lots of men come knockin' at my trailer door. Usually they're there to read the meter, collect on a bill, or just get directions to Faye Faye's trailer, the slut, but from time to time it happens to be men who want to be entertained by me. Bein' the lady that I am, I make 'em wait outside until I've lit a few candles and made a pass or two through the trailer with the Glade can. But when I do let 'em in I always feel that I owe 'em somethin' nice, but since I don't know how long they're actually stayin' and don't want to waste the good booze on brief encounters, I always make 'em my special champagne cocktail recipe. This stuff is so good, they don't know that I ain't actually popped open a bottle of the Cook's or André stuff I keep locked up in my secret liquor cabinet. That stuff only comes out when I know for sure that he's a winner, at least for that night. So anyhow, this stuff will work its magic for you, and your husband's boss won't be any the wiser.

## Donna Sue's Trailer Park Champagne Cocktail

Makes about 10 to 12 servin's

- ⅔ cup water
- ⅔ cup sugar
- 1 cup grapefruit juice
- ½ cup orange juice
- 3 tablespoons grenadine
- 28 ounces cheap champagne, chilled
- sugar cubes (optional)

Put a saucepan over low heat and add the water and sugar. Stir until the sugar dissolves completely and then let it reach a boil. Boil for 10 minutes, stirrin' occasionally. Pour it into a large pot and add the grapefruit juice and orange juice. Stir well and put covered in the fridge for an hour to two. When you're ready to serve the beverage, add the grenadine and the cheap chilled champagne and stir. Serve in champagne flute glasses if your guests ain't too drunk to break 'em. And feel free to pop a sugar cube into each glass just to give it the right look if you want.

May Your Glasses Be Full, and Your Bottoms Up,
Donna Sue Boxcar

# Chapter 7

# Etiquette

*The men at the High Chaparral Trailer Park proudly display their balls. From left to right are Kenny Lynn of Lot #15, Donny Owens of Lot #15, Kyle Chitwood of Lot #11, Mickey Ray Kay of Lot #13, and Harland Hix of Lot #9.*

If there's one sport that's loved and actively played by folks in trailer parks all around the world, it'd have to be bowlin'. Now I know that some of y'all would've guessed miniature golf, race car drivin', or even wrestlin', but I'm sorry to say you'd been wrong. You see, even though those three athletic doin's are popular with people who live in trailer parks, you got to take into consideration the fact that not everybody can participate in 'em. For example, I know that even though my Me-Ma used to love to go to Putt-Putt, with her eyesight the way it is now, the last time we took her to play, the only balls she seemed to be able to hit with that rented putter were the ones in my husband's pants and then those got caught in the windmill. And when it comes to race car drivin,' we're lucky to get to work and back without that piece of junk that our "mechanically declined" husbands keep tryin' to rebuild. And considerin' that the last time I tried wrestlin' somebody, he ended up in the hospital for two days (by the way, my husband, Dew, says thanks for all those thoughtful cards and flowers that y'all was kind enough to send). No, those three sports are what we folks call "fantasy events." When we watch 'em on TV, we fantasize that we was the ones gettin' our balls in the clown's mouth, or drivin' that winnin' lap with the checkered flag, or even pullin' a clothesline on that fat-mouthed son of a trash heap in tights. But when it comes to actually breakin' into a sweat in a sportin' activity, it'd have to be bowlin'. One of the reasons for this is that everybody, regardless if they're fat or thin, short or tall, rich or poor, young or old, sittin' in a wheelchair or walkin' with a walker, blind or with 20/20 vision, good-lookin' or dog-ugly, can bowl. Why I saw this one armless gal on TV not too long back that was bowlin' with her feet. She'd throw that ball usin' just her toes, and I tell ya'll she was as good as anybody up at the Great Big Balls Bowling Alley. Yes, even my own Me-Ma can enjoy the thrill of bowlin', just as long as we find her a six-pound ball and aim her in the right direction with a long stick.

It's on account of bowlin' bein' an every-man-woman-and-child activity that you find the use of just plain old terrible etiquette goin' on in practically near any bowlin' alley. It seems that folks just don't know how to act correctly from the time they walk in the door of their favorite bowlin' establishment to the time they walk out. And I'm not just talkin' about when to bowl, or who goes first, or even who keeps the score. No, it goes even further than that, which is why I've selected this trailer park pastime as the subject for this chapter. After all, I think we all want to be on our toes when we kick back a few and throw gigantic heavy objects in the air. We want to enjoy the athletic sport of bowlin' just like the family down on the next lane, but we just don't know what we're doin' wrong. But not to worry or lose sleep over the matter, 'cause you were smart enough to buy this book, or lucky enough to have someone that cares for you to buy it for you.

In this chapter we're gonna hit all the big mistakes that I see takin' place every time I stop in at one of the many bowlin' alleys across the globe to throw ten or twenty frames. These are errors that even some of the new folks who've moved into the area and now call the Great Big Balls Bowling Alley their own tend to make from time to time. I'll hit everythin' from the small traditional mistakes to the great big blunders that bowlers keep pullin' off. You'll see things in a different light that, once I've brought 'em up to the front and have gone over 'em, will amaze and astonish you that you were ever doin' 'em like you did in the first place. But most important, you'll be able to join a group of friends for a game of bowlin'or even join a bowlin' league with the assurance that you're doin' everythin' right and without the worry of missin' out on any of the fun. So, let's get started.

## Carryin' a Ball

If you bring a ball with you to the bowlin' alley like most of us do, don't expect someone else to carry it from the car to the lane or vice versa. There's no reason on God's green earth that my husband, Dew, should get a hernia or throw a disk causin' our team to bowl badly just 'cause he has to carry both his ball and mine. I don't care if you're 109 years old and know Willard Scott personally; if you bring your own ball, then you carry it around. Just think of it this way, when it comes to balls in the game of bowlin', there are no men or women, but only opponents. So once again, let me make this clear as clear can be—if you brung it, you carry it.

## Gettin' Luck from the Trophy Case

You wouldn't believe all the stuff I've seen when it comes to the trophy cases that are found in bowlin' alleys everywhere. For some reason folks have got it in their heads that if they salute, bow down to, rosin, rub, spit at, touch their ball to, or even genuflect or pray in front of an award-filled bowlin' trophy case that somehow magically good luck will shine upon 'em that night when they begin to throw. Folks, let me tell you right here and now that all those acts are both a waste of time as well as a crock of bull. None of these activities will give you a better game, an edge over your opponent, or even a quicker ball return. There is no good luck charm that comes from them publicly displayed trophy cases, unless of course you kiss 'em. That's right, all you got to do is just kiss the case when you first come in and you're sure to bowl one of the best games ever. Now, there ain't no need to make out with the case. A little tongue action ain't gonna get you a perfect game. All you need to do is press your lips to the case and give it a little peck. That's it. It couldn't be no simpler than that. So do us all a favor and leave your voodoo crap at home. Just kiss the case and walk on so we all can get a chance to throw a practice ball or two without havin' to wait for you to do your stupid trophy dance that ain't gonna do nothin' for you anyways.

One more thing on this topic before we move on, and that is that the trophy case luck doesn't care what kind of car you drive, ball you throw, or trailer you live in. It gives out its luck on a first-come basis. So if your team bowls like a drunken sailor on a Tuesday night in Flagstaff, then that means that either all of your opponents' team members got there before yours did, or somebody on your team either forgot to kiss the case or tried to get a little too fresh with it. So blame them, not the case. It can't be held responsible for stupidity.

## Tippin' the Shoe Boy

I don't know where or in what realm of the world this new habit has come from, but let me tell y'all that it's just wrong, wrong, wrong to tip a shoe boy! You should never tip a shoe boy at anytime for anything. It could lead to some kind of crazy ritual where you have to tip all the way up to the fellow who assigns and turns on your lanes. Now it's all right to flirt with the shoe boy if it means that he might give them there rented shoes an extra squirt of that antifungus spray or maybe even get you the employee discount on an order of cheese fries at the concession stand. And if he likes you a lot, why you might even get a pair of shoes that fit. So just remember, it's OK to sleep with the shoe boy for favors, but never ever tip him.

Ladies, if the shoe boy happens to be a shoe girl, well just shut the heck up and take whatever she gives you with a smile. Just remember, one of these days after that rude gum-chewin', low-cut-blouse-wearin' skank gets fired from the bowlin' alley, your foot and her butt have a date.

## Changin' Shoes

Always change your shoes before doin' anything else. There's nothin' worse than comin' down into the seatin' area with your arms full of selected items from the concession stand and trippin' over some bozo who is finally puttin' on his doggone bowlin' shoes. I'll kick you into next year's league if you do this to me. So as soon as you've found your lane, sit your happy behind down and change your shoes.

And please take your street shoes and place 'em in a locker. For some reason some folks think it's OK to just leave their shoes tucked under the seats. These are the same folks that think they can eat onions and garlic and not have to take a Tic Tac. Folks, regardless of what fictional world you might be livin' in, let me assure you that your feet stink. I don't care if you can smell 'em or not, they do. For some unknown reason all them God-fearin' Baptists who enjoy a good friendly game at the Great Big Balls Bowling Alley over by where I live are happy to quote you a scripture passage if they think you might have run out to your car to down a beer, but they sure can't remember the verse where our savior washed the feet of his disciples. I don't think some of them folks' feet have seen water since the day they was baptized, but nonetheless, they'll still leave their sardine-smellin' shoes right there for everyone to gag on. Needless to say, I don't put up with it and neither should anyone else that happens to be bowlin' with you. So, please, do us all a favor and either put those nasty hoof covers in a locker or place 'em under the seats of the team with the highest scores, just as long as y'all ain't playin' 'em that night. And if you ain't in a league, then you got only one choice—go get a locker, for cryin' out loud.

And another thing, I don't care if you wore flip-flops to the bowlin' alley, put some socks on before you slip on those rented shoes. Nobody wants to wear a pair after you've finished with 'em if you ain't got no socks, panty hose, or knee-highs on your stinky feet, regardless of how many times those shoes get sprayed down and sanitized. Just put a pair of extra socks in your glove box. That way if you forget to wear any, you'll always have a pair in your car. Just make sure to change 'em out once or twice a year.

## Two Balls Is Enough

Before you even start on pickin' a ball, I want to clear up somethin' that lots of people seem to misunderstand. When you're watchin' them professional bowlers compete for the big money on TV, y'all might notice that there are several balls restin' in the ball rack. That's on account of the fact that these high bowlers use their balls kind of like golfers use their clubs. They got certain ones that will go left, right, forward, spin this way or that way, or whichever way they need 'em to go. And yes, these are great pieces of equipment to have if you're goin' for big money, but, folks, if you only play your friends or family or are even in a league, twelve balls is too many. My sister, Donna Sue, likes to have twelve balls when she plays, but that's for another reason. You see, she starts off with a light one, but as her drinkin' continues she moves on to the heavier ones in order to keep her balance and stop from fallin' over. As the night and the booze go on, she switches from ball to ball, so that if she's stumblin' to the left she can bowl with a ball that hooks to the right in order to throw a strike and vice versa. If she didn't have all them balls, then she wouldn't be able to play the entire night. But she is an exception to the rule. Well, she and my mother in-law, Momma Ballzak, are the exceptions to the rule. All the rest of us ain't got no need for more than two balls in that ball rack at any given time. Any amount over two balls is just downright ball gluttony or a need for men to publicly make up in the areas that they're lackin' in, if you know what I mean. That's why my husband usually bowls with a little girl's ball, but trust me when I tell y'all he could just as easily get a strike with a Ping-Pong ball. Yes, the good Lord has blessed me with looks, talent, and a husband who could play pool without a cue. God bless him, he's always had real strong fingers.

## Selectin' Your Ball

When it comes to rental ball selectin', I got to be honest and tell y'all that the folks up at the High Chaparral Trailer Park ain't all that good at it. You see, all of 'em got their own balls, includin' me. Of course with my busy schedule and all, I ain't got the time to be on a team, but when I am in town, everybody wants me to sub 'cause with my handicap, we just blow the other team away. But there are a few traditional tips to remember when selectin' a rental ball for yourself.

**1.** A heavy ball ain't always the best ball to choose. This is true since with all that weight your arm is sure to get tired way before the tenth frame, and you're most likely gonna end up throwin' some bad balls. So just because you happen to be a big masculine man don't mean you got to use a sixteen-pound ball. Drop down to a twelve- or fourteen-pound ball and prove your manhood with your score instead. Of course sometimes it's hard findin' a sixteen-pound ball when them out-of-town ladies leagues are bowlin' our gals over at the Great Big Balls Bowling Alley.

**2.** Always be careful to check before you put your fingers in strange holes since you never know whose hand was in there before or what kinda thing might be in there now. That's one of the reasons that I don't lend my ball out to nobody.

**3.** Make sure to clean your rental balls. Now, if you own your balls, then most likely you clean 'em on a regular basis. This unfortunately ain't true when it comes to those rental balls. As a matter of fact, they almost never get cleaned, so you can only imagine the amount of built-up grime that must be on those poor things. Especially when you consider how many times they get used in a week, thrown down those oiled lanes, kicked up by that nasty ball return, and then groped by human hands. Can you just imagine how nasty your own balls would be if you didn't clean 'em yourself? So after selectin' the rental ball or balls that you'll be throwin' that night, make sure to either clean 'em yourself or let someone else clean 'em for you. There are always folks out there that will be happy to give you a hand. Why, my sister, Donna Sue, has personally cleaned more balls in this part of the state than any other person dead or alive. Although her good friend and coworker Little Linda has to be a close second. I know that both these gals volunteered to take care of all the balls for the men's league this past year. Needless to say, the fellows were eruptin' with excitement after Donna Sue and Little Linda got hold of their balls. Why, they even credit the ball cleanin' my sister and Little Linda did to the record-breakin' high scores that the fellows had at the Great Big Balls Bowling Alley. So the next time you get ready to bowl, make sure you either put your balls in one of those cleanin' machines or simply give 'em an old spit and shine. Trust me when I say that your balls will thank you.

**4.** Avoid depressed balls. You want your balls to have a nice round surface free from depressions, chips, and grooves. Trust me when I tell y'all that good bowlers ain't got groovy balls.

**5.** Make sure that your hand spread is comfortable. You don't want the holes to be too far apart from each other or you could strain your hand. You want your holes to be accessible. So once you've followed rule number 2, and have checked to make sure that the holes are clean, go ahead and stick your fingers in. Can you pick the ball up easily? Do you find that you keep fallin' out of the holes? The last thing you want to do is make your approach only to fall out of the holes. Not only can that be embarrassin', but it can also be very dangerous. But if the spread feels great and you're not havin' any problems with the holes, then go ahead and try a practice shot with it.

**6.** And last but not least, if you don't like the balls you're bowlin' with, feel free to change 'em anytime durin' the game just as long as you don't hold up the action.

## Concession Stand Manners

Now, when it comes to us trailer park folks, the concession stand is like a holy shrine for us, second to none in that bowlin' alley, includin' the usually dark and seedy cocktail lounge. Even my sister will choose the concession stand over the bowlin' alley bar. Of course she always brings three or four fully loaded flasks and a minibar in that second bowlin' bag she carts around when she plays. Donna Sue also says that you have more of a selection of, and I'm quotin', "hot daddies" at the concession stand than you do in the bar. I personally would've thought she'd do better when it comes to pickin' up men in the bar area on account of the fact that it is so dark and dimly lit.

I guess the reasonin' for our high appreciation for the snack shack is simply that regardless of how bad you might be bowlin', you can always run up and grab some chili cheese nachos for comfort. Lord knows you ain't gonna be the only gutter-ball-throwin' patron in line. And, of course, that's why your behavior and trailer park manners are so important when you're gettin' a bite to eat.

Just remember that regardless of how hungry you might get, you are at the bowlin' alley to bowl first and eat second. This means that at no time should your longin' desire for a soft pretzel with cheese keep your teammates waitin' to throw their balls. This is why I always suggest that as soon as you've put on your shoes and placed your personal or rental bowlin' ball in the ball rack, go hit the concession stand and load up. Get as much of your food as you can on that first go around. There is no reason to grab a corn dog before you bowl only to later find yourself runnin' to the concession stand every three frames for more delectable goodies. That, simply put, is borderline manual labor/exercise, and we sure ain't come to the bowlin' alley for that. So try to plan out what you want to eat by the time you pull into the parkin' lot, and keep to that menu.

At most bowlin' alleys you'll typically order your food and either give your name to the person behind the counter (make sure you give 'em your full name so someone else with the name Boxcar or Ruby Ann don't mistakenly pick up your food) or they'll give you a piece of paper with a number on it. Unlike dinin' at a restaurant, you ain't got to hang around the counter for them to call your name. Instead, you can go back to the lanes you're playin' on and start warmin' up with a few practice throws. By now you're old enough to recognize your name over a loudspeaker or memorize that number they gave you. You can do two things at once, and if you can't, don't worry, 'cause you ain't gonna miss out on your food. Worst case scenario is that they have to call your name or number a few times before you hear it.

## Wearin' a Glove

Now, this is a question that you have to answer for yourself. The whole purpose of puttin' on a glove is to stop you from turnin' your hand when you release the ball. So if you need that kind of help, then I say yes, go for it. Of course nobody down at the Great Big Balls Bowling Alley wears a glove. As a matter of fact, the pro shop don't even sell 'em. We just use duct tape around our wrists and hands. That stuff works just as good as one of them expensive gloves. Of course, the menfolk all got these places on their wrist and hands that they ain't got no hair on anymore, but hey, that's the cost of bein' a good athlete. Just make sure that if you're ever bowlin' at the Great Big Balls Bowling Alley you bring your own duct tape. The pro shop charges $4.95 for a little old roll of that silver stuff.

## When and What to Rosin

You know, it's these young pups or egotistical bowlers that give rosin a bad name. These folks wear that white powdery stuff all over 'em just so folks will think they know what they're doin'. Some of 'em have got that stuff all the way up to their dang elbows for cryin' out loud. Y'all know the folks I'm talkin' about. They show up to the alley with their own shoes, ball, and freshly laundered bowlin' towel. Then they take out their little rosin bag and get to poundin' on that thing till they look like Pig Pen from Peanuts with all that cloud of dust surroundin' 'em. And then they still can't break 100! I put them on my prayer list too, askin' that God hit 'em upside the head with some kind of sense.

The whole purpose of the rosin bag is to help you get a better grip by dryin' out your hands and eliminatin' any moisture you might have on 'em before you pick up your ball. So, I say use it if you want, but you only need to do your hands and just before you get ready to throw your ball. Of course when the nursing home makes us take her out and we already got a lane reserved, my poor Me-Ma's hands are so doggone dry that we always make her put on some lotion first to give us all a fair playin' field. God bless her, one night she put her hands over that blower that they got on the ball rack and her dry skin just went flyin' all up in the air. You'd have thought she'd released a handful of confetti, for cryin' out loud. Why, I had her over for supper the other day and asked her if she'd help me clean up by brushin' the crumbs off the table with her hands. When I went to refinish that kitchen table later that day I was able to skip the sandin'-it-down part completely on account of her hands bein' so dang dry.

## How Many Practice Balls Should You Throw

When it comes to practice or warm-up throws, there really ain't no rule. Go ahead and throw as many as you like, but just do a frame's worth at a time. For example, if you get a strike, then go ahead and let someone else throw a practice frame. Or if you throw one ball and knock down a few, then go ahead and throw a second ball to try and pick up the ones that are standin'. Then go set down and wait your turn. Or, you can always come early and throw a few without the constant worry of havin' someone breathin' down your back. Just make sure you don't throw all your good balls first. The last thing you want to do is bowl your good game when it don't count. And if the bowlin' alley insists that you pay for an additional game, you might want to cut back a few throws.

## Whose Name Goes First on the Score Sheet?

Now, there ain't no real set rule that I know of on this topic. When you're playin' as teams, then you alternate between the players of each team. Joe from team one might go first, then someone from team two would go next, followed by someone else from team one. It would just keep goin' like that. Of course if it's just a group of people bowlin', then the rule of thumb at the Great Big Balls Bowling Alley is that you go in alphabetical order, which basically means, for example, that Donna Lee would be listed before Donna Lynn or Donna Sue. Personally I don't mind where I end up in the order, just as long as I get to play.

## Who Keeps Score?

Most bowlin' alleys in today's world have computers that do it all for you. With that said, there are still some alleys like the Great Big Balls Bowling Alley that rely on the players to keep track of their own tallies. This always makes it a bit difficult since someone has to keep track of the scores, but who? Well, what we do is pick out the two folks who can actually do arithmetic and multiplication. Sometimes that tends to be a difficult task, and when the time arises that we ain't got nobody that can, then we simply ask the neighborin' team if they'd be so kind as to help us. I'm usually the one that keeps the score whenever I bowl. Thank the Lord I keep a calculator with me at all times.

## Who Bowls First?

Now, this question is easy. The first person on the score sheet bowls first, and when we all play they start on the right lane first. The right lane always has the right of way just like in drivin'. This means that when two bowlers come up to bowl with one on each lane, the one on the right always goes first. So make sure that you check to your left and to your right to see if you happen to be the one on the right. Just 'cause your group is bowlin' on lanes three and four, don't think that lane four is always the right lane, 'cause it's not when you consider that the folks over in lane two think that lane number three is the right lane.

## Somethin' to Remember When It's Your Turn

You ain't got to get up there after you've lined your feet up and got your arrow in sight, just to take fifteen minutes before you throw your dang ball. Good Lord, folks, this ain't a prayer vigil. Some of y'all would think you was throwin' a bomb rather than a ball. If you can't just get up there, aim, and throw your ball, then maybe you might try some other sport where people ain't involved. Maybe pinball.

## Your Lane

When we bowl we usually take up two lanes, which we alternate between. Please try to keep this in mind when you throw your ball. I hate it when somebody goes up and throws their ball only to wind up with their legs spread all out and into your approach area. I'm the first to agree that each person has to find his own bowlin' style, but trust me when I say that if you got your leg in my way when it's my turn to bowl, you're gonna need a doctor and a cast. So go ahead and do that funky chicken approach of yours, but just be careful where your dance ends.

## Controllin' Your Emotions

I know some folks will tell you to be professional when you're out there bowlin', but I'm sorry, if you get a strike or pick up a spare, then go ahead and let it all hang out. If this means whoppin' and hollerin' a little bit, then so be it. After all, this just might be the only thing good that happens to y'all for the whole year. Of course, gettin' mad and kickin' things or throwin' your rosin bag ain't nothin' but stupid. It's only a game.

## When to Use the Blower

Now, that blower is there to help you dry off your hands. It's kind of like usin' the rosin, but not as messy, or as good for that matter. Personally the only thing I use it for is to blow a little life back into an order of cheese fries that have coagulated. But when it comes to the game of bowlin', just like the rosin, this is really only needed to be used just before you get ready to throw your ball. But since it's only air, feel free to use it anytime you like. Just don't try to be like Little Linda and blame that occasional offensive smell on the blower.

## When to Use the Return Button

Normally the pin-settin' machine will come down, pick up the remainin' pins, if any, and then as it rises up the sweep bar will clear all the pins you knocked down out of the way and into the pit, and then the machine will lower down your remainin' pins for you to play. If your ball hasn't returned once this cycle is over, then go ahead and think about usin' the ball return button. Just make sure you tell everyone that your ball has not returned and get their approval on you pushin' the button. Don't push it if not everyone agrees that you should. If they want to wait a bit more, then so be it. I say this on account of the fact that once that return button has been hit, the machine will recycle the pins and you'll have to start all over again. Some of the folks you're bowlin' with may not be real keen on this idea. So even though it ain't the launch button for nuclear missiles, it should be treated just like it is.

## When to Use the Cocktail Waitress Call Button

Accordin' to my sister, Donna Sue, you should only use this button when "you've mistakenly misjudged the amount of liquor you'd need for your bowlin' experience." She also adds that you should never push it if you don't need it. "The last thing you want to have happen is to cry wolf so many times that when you really do need her she don't come." She broke into a sweat durin' that last sentence.

## The Beer Frame

Typically the seventh frame is known as the beer frame, and it's either the person with the lowest score at the end of that frame or the person who bowls the worst in that frame that has to buy everyone a beer. Y'all will need to decide which way y'all are playin' this one and if you're gonna play it at all. At the Great Big Balls Bowling Alley we don't waste time with beer, after all, we got a whole twelve-pack out in the car if we want it. So the seventh frame is traditionally known in our parts as the "beer-battered-onion-ring frame."

So if y'all just follow these simple steps of proper etiquette the next time you pull your ball out of the closet, I'm sure everyone down at the bowlin' alley is sure to have a good clean afternoon or evenin' of fun.

## Ask Ruby Ann . . .

Dear Ruby Ann,

I'm in a league and really enjoy bowling, but I have to admit that I don't have a whole lot of money to spend. The dues alone put me right at the edge of my budget. So I don't have a lot of money to spend on soft drinks or beer when we bowl. Do you think it would be all right if I brought my own beverages and food to the alley?

Shanna A.<br>Toronto, Canada

Dear Shanna,

Bringin' your own food and drinks to a bowlin' alley for a game is like bringin' your own crackers and grape juice to church for Communion. If you want somethin' from the concession stand, then all you got to do is flirt. That's right, flirt around with the menfolk in the bowlin' alley. Make yourself out to be a fun person to talk to. Why, men will be buyin' anythin' you want if it means gettin' a chance to talk to you. And don't worry about how attractive you are either when you're out there flirtin'. After all, my sister, Donna Sue, is able to win some poor man every night, so it can be done. So grab that tight shirt or low-cut blouse the next time you go bowlin'. You might even pretend that you need help carryin' your ball or your shoes. Make yourself look like you are in need of some kind of assistance. That should do the trick.

So just use what the good Lord done gave you, and pray that you bowl against some Lutherans. Them folks are known to pass out the beers regardless of what you look like or who you are.

Love, Kisses, and Trailer Park Wishes,
Ruby Ann Boxcar

# Chapter 8

# Indoor Flower Arrangin'

*If this lovely wall floral arrangement—which was quickly assembled by usin' a hot glue gun, a hospital bed pan, and some plastic flowers that we brought back home after Mamma's recent overnight hospital stay for an enlarged corn removal—don't show y'all how easy and simple it is to beautify your trailer with synthetic vegetation, then nothin' will.*

You know nothin' says pure class like plastic flower arrangements strategically located in your trailer home. Not only are they a sign of good livin', but they also bring a feelin' of elegance to your trailer. But it seems like the fine art of arrangin' and even creatin' a beautiful bouquet assortment is fadin' away almost as fast as the aroma that these modern miracles of science give off if you don't give 'em a good blast at least once a month durin' winter and every other week durin' the warmer parts of the year with that concentrated fragrance spray. And for some reason you just don't see that many byproduct-petaled groupin's when you go callin' on your neighbors. Nowadays people have traded the beauty of a nice display of synthetic flowers for real plants that you got to water and take care of or they'll die. I think the reason for this is the myth that plastic flowers take too much time to keep pretty. Why, a weekly dustin' is just fine for keepin' my stunnin' simulated adornments on the side of loveliness. I just think people need to be retrained or, as in the case for some folks, trained for the very first time in the art of livin' with plastic flowers and the joys that they can bring. But not to worry, 'cause once again I'm about to come through for y'all.

There is one particular subject that I'd like to quickly cover in this chapter. It seems that folks are always askin' me where they can find good plastic flowers, and I totally understand why they ask. It seems like for one reason or another, the people who decide on what kind of flowers to make are leanin' stronger and stronger towards silk or satin artificial flowers, makin' it near impossible to find good-lookin' plastic ones anywhere. This just goes to show that my teacher, Mr. Willybuster, was wrong when he tried to teach us about that supply-and-demand theory of his. So now we people of taste have to find a new source for our arrangements. Well, once again, I've got the answer. Believe it or not, cemeteries seem to display some of the best-lookin' plastic flowers that you can find in today's world. Of course, this leads us back to the florist who makes these wonderful gravesite arrangements. But here is where we get into a bit of a problem. I've found that the florist won't sell you just a bunch of plastic flowers, so you have to buy an arrangement, which the price alone will take you straight to bankruptcy court. So what are we left to do? Well, I don't know about y'all, but I just go to the cemetery and take a few handfuls when I feel like makin' a new arrangement for my trailer. Now I know that to some of y'all, that sounds morbid and just plain old un-Christian-like. I'm sure some of y'all are even cryin' out, "Thief," but that couldn't be further from the truth. In order to steal somethin' it's got to belong to somebody. With that in mind, who do these cemetery flowers belong to? They ain't property of the cemetery, and the folks who originally bought 'em just up and left 'em there like they would a paper cup or an empty potato chip bag. And I don't know about where you live, but in my state they encourage us folks to join in and pick up trash whenever we see it. Do your part to keep this country of ours beautiful by helpin' to clean up our cemeteries. Of course you might want to do your trash pickin' up closer to around 5:00 A.M., when the sheriff is over at the House of Holes Donut Hut enjoyin' a few cream-filled long johns.

So now that you got the skinny on plastic flowers, grab a vase and let's get to beautifyin' your home.

## Centerpiece

As I mentioned in Chapter 4, havin' a centerpiece for your dinner table is very important. It shows that you got both class and taste as it sets there makin' your home beautiful. Though you can use just about anything for a centerpiece, I personally like mine to be floral, 'cause not only are the plastic flowers beautiful on a properly set dinner table, but if you get food on your plastic centerpiece, you can just wipe it down with a damp sponge. Now, you can go three ways with your tabletop creation: themed, personal, or generic.

Themed centerpieces can make or break a dinner. Regardless of how bad the food is, which of course it never is in a trailer park, if your centerpiece is real nice, everyone will remember that part of the dinner regardless how many bottles of Pepto-Bismol they go through afterwards. An example of a themed centerpiece would be the one that Lois Bunch used when she had me and my husband over to dine just last month. Since Lois was servin' us a big Tex-Mex make-your-own taco and burrito meal, she went with a Mexican theme for her table. She took an old sombrero and put flowers all along the outside of the brim. She then covered the top of the hat with some beautiful plastic flowers. She took some foil and filled the inside of the brim with it, and then she put taco/burrito meat in there. What great fun me, my husband, Dew, and the rest of the guests had spoonin' out the meat for our tacos and burritos right from the hat. Needless to say, that old worn-out hat was the hit of the party. It was simple to make, but it sure made a big difference and added a flair to the theme.

A centerpiece that falls into the realm of personal is one that shares a little bit about you, your spouse, or just your household. Since me and my husband love country music, I decided to use that part of us for a big Italian dinner I'd prepared when we had a few friends over one night. So I took an old boot that I'd seen one day when I was helpin' my sister and Little Linda pick up trash along the highway (no, I was not wearin' one of them orange jumpsuits, since only the people doin' community service are allowed one of them). I took a paper towel and some spray cleaner and cleaned the outside of the boot before addin' a few flowers here and there. I set it on the dinner table and stuck a loaf of French bread in it. When my guests wanted a piece of the bread, they'd just rip a hunk off right from the boot. I tell you, folks had such a good time retrievin' that bread out of there that they done forgot it wasn't garlic bread. You should have seen 'em tryin' to dig that last little end piece out of the toe end of the boot. And I had a great time with the whole thing as well. Why, my niece, Lulu Bell, recently gave me another old boot that she couldn't find the mate to. I plan to take the flowers off my first boot, spray-paint 'em red since they don't match, and put flowers on both of 'em. That way I can use 'em as centerpieces and bread holders for when I entertain larger groups of people. And I'm thinkin' about turnin' a pair of my late Pa-Pa's bowlin' shoes into centerpieces/gravy boats if I can find a way to patch up them holes. I might however, just have to drop the gravy boat idea and simply go with my original idea of centerpieces/margarine holders.

Despite what bland and unemotional images might come to mind when you think of the word "generic," this type of centerpiece can be both excitin' and beautiful. The only difference between this kind and the other two that we mentioned is that any old object will do when you're selectin' one to be decorated. Why, I attended a dinner at Opal Lamb-Inman's trailer where she'd taken and glued assorted flowers all over an old red wagon that Tammy Cantrell had left under the trailer when she moved away with all her dang kids. Opal took the big handle off and put a rope where it had been and another one on the other end or back of the wagon. Then she put the casserole and side dishes inside it. When the guests were ready to serve themselves they'd simply tell Opal or her husband, Dick, who of course were seated at the ends of the table, and whichever one was closest to 'em would pull on the rope, causin' the wagon to roll down to that end of the dinner table. It was really creative yet simple. And since it didn't go along with a theme or show the guest anything personal about Opal or Dick, it fell into the category of bein' a generic centerpiece. And as you can guess, even though Opal's wagon was generic, the last thing it was was bland or borin'. Of course if I'd done it, I'd have made sure to clean the inside of the wagon out real good so to ensure that none of the rust or paint chips, which we later found out at the hospital contained lead, were able to get into the food. But that's just me.

Now that you got an idea of what you can do when it comes to creatin' your own centerpiece, I thought I'd show you how to make my boot that I mentioned earlier. It's real easy and very crafty. If you ain't got a spare boot that you can use, then call up your friends and neighbors or just go to your local trash dump or if you ain't got that kind of time, stop off at a nearby thrift store.

# Boot Centerpiece

**SUPPLIES**

Boot
Paper towel
Bottle cleaner
Can of disinfectant
2 sheets of newspaper (1 sheet is optional)
Can of spray paint (optional)
Hot glue gun
Hot glue sticks
Plastic flowers

**1.** Take your boot and shake it out real good.

**2.** Usin' the paper towel and cleaner, wipe the outside of your boot down real good.

**3.** Give the inside of the boot a good blast of disinfectant spray, and then set the boot aside to dry for 30 minutes.

**4.** Once it's dried on the outside, place it on a sheet of newspaper. If you decide to spray-paint your boot, continue. If not, skip to number 6.

**5.** Take the second sheet of newspaper, lightly crumple it up, and place it in the top of the boot so that you can't look into the boot but the paper still sticks out. This way when you spray-paint the boot, none of the inside will get painted. Now give your boot a good coat of paint. If you want to take the time to tape off the heel and sole so they don't get painted, so be it, but that is strictly up to you. Set the boot aside and let it dry for 1 to 2 hours, then take out the stuffed newspaper.

**6.** Plug in your hot glue gun and let it rest on the newspaper so the little that might drip out don't get on nothin'.

**7.** Once the glue gun is ready to be used, decide where you would like your flowers to go.

**8.** One at a time, place a little glue on the back of a flower and then press it against the boot until it sticks. You might want to brace the boot when you place the flower on it by simply slidin' your free hand into the boot and applyin' pressure on the same area inside where you're pushin' the flower to on the outside.

**9.** Once you've placed the few flowers where you want 'em, set the boot aside and let dry.

Now your boot is ready for a loaf of bread to be stuck down in it. And all that for just a few pennies or dollars to say the least. I do hope y'all will try other items to put flowers on when makin' your centerpieces. As a matter of fact, I'd love to see what kind of creations you come up with. Please take a photo and send it to my publisher or e-mail it directly to me at rubylot18@aol.com. I can't wait to see your handiwork.

## Trailer Floral Arrangements

I've found that plastic flowers ain't just for dinner anymore. As a matter of fact, I like to take 'em and place homemade arrangements throughout my trailer. Now, even as I say this, I know that some of y'all are gonna go out, get artificial flowers, stick 'em in a vase, and call it a day. Well, that ain't what I'm talkin' about. Anybody can do that. No, I'm findin' that personalized handcrafted vases containin' a lovely fake flower arrangement make a simple, yet lively accent to brighten up that trailer home of yours. Yes, dear reader, you can be as creative with your vase makin' as you were with makin' your centerpiece. The only thing is that there's only one kind of style when it comes to makin' a floral arrangement in a home with wheels, and that is the personal-style method. We toss out both the generic, since we want it to be more of an expression of ourselves, and the theme style, even though we can make it a personal arrangement that goes with the motif of our home.

One example that comes to mind right off the bat when we talk about personal method is the vase that Juanita Hix of Lot #9 made by simply hot-gluin' both her daughters, Harlinda and Bonita's baby pictures to an old small coffee can. She also hot-glued pink yarn around the can to give it that special baby-girl feel. It was very cute and the talk of the park for a good long time.

Even my sister, Donna Sue, was so inspired by Juanita's vase that she went out and made her own from a coffee can, a hot glue gun, and a six-pack of empty beer cans. It was lovely and the whole project would've cost her next to nothin' if she hadn't had to call out the volunteer fire department for help after she'd accidentally glued her entire butt to the sofa. I don't know how many times I've told my tipsy sister to never do crafts naked.

Since I love country music as y'all already know, I recently made a vase as a gift for one of my favorite singers of all time, Reba McEntire. It was easy to make, and it turned out so pretty. I packed it up and sent it to her only to find it back on my doorstep the followin' week. I don't know what happened, but the box had been opened and then taped back up, and there was no note or nothin' on it at all. So I just put more postage on it and sent it back to her again. You know that box went and came back a total of six more times until finally on the outside in big black magic marker, somebody wrote the words "PLEASE KEEP THIS" on it. From the way it looked, Reba or one of her people must have thought I'd spent a lot of money on that vase, and so they couldn't accept it. Of course, I was honored by that, and I completely understood. So I got it settin' in my office next to the glass box of Reba hair that I bought off of eBay from a hotel maid who after Reba had checked out, had had the good sense to pull it out of the bathroom trash when she was cleanin' the room.

# Cowboy Hat Vase

Since my Reba gift vase was so easy to make, I thought maybe it'd be the perfect as well as cheapest one that we could make. This craft will give you an idea of what you can do when it comes to homemade vases for plastic flowers. I know that you're gonna love this one as much as me and Reba's people do.

**SUPPLIES**

Cowboy hat—get one down at the thrift store, and you can even spray-paint it if you want it to match the colors in your house
Scissors
Cheap flimsy pie pan
Florist Styrofoam
Plastic flowers
Big letter (optional)
Hot glue (optional)

**1.** Take your cowboy hat and carefully cut off the very top of it.

**2.** Insert the pie pan from the bottom of the hat. You will have to bend the pan out of shape, which is why you want a real flimsy one. Push the pan as far up as you can.

**3.** Next, put your hand through the top of the hat and push the pan back down until the bottom of the pan is even with the bottom of the hat. It's all right if the sides of the pan are bent up.

**4.** Insert the florist Styrofoam and then add your plastic flowers. The pie pan will hold the whole thing together if you have to pick it up and move it.

**5.** If you want you can hot-glue a big iron-on letter on the front of the hat. My Reba hat has a big red R on it, but this letter and even puttin' any letter on the front is optional.

Now there ain't no reason not to have somethin' pretty, plastic, and floral in your trailer home. Just go with your own personal taste and likes. After all, as I've said many times, you're the one who has to live with it. You know, now that I think of it, the same thing can be said for men and pets. Of course a lovely plastic floral arrangement won't cheat on you or eat up your good shoes.

## Ask Ruby Ann . . .

Dear Ruby Ann,

Is there ever a good time to use real flowers?

Elaine and Ken
Phoenix, Arizona

Dear Elaine and Ken,

What a wonderful question. Since we trailer park folks are always considerate and think of others, we never use anythin' but plastic flowers inside our trailers. The last thing you want is a guest to stop by who's allergic to flowers or pollen or such. So the answer to your question is no, there never is a good time to use real flowers inside your house. And after sayin' that I got to come back and say that my mother in-law, Momma Ballzak, does like to use real flowers from time to time, but the only person that ever comes over to her trailer is Donna Sue, and that's for a snort of hooch. She could have a great big man-eatin' Venus fly trap in there and my sister would still stop by as long as a free drink or two was on the agenda.

Now, there is a time when we trailer folk people always use real flowers, and that's when someone has passed away. Then and only then will we leave real flowers at their gravesite 'cause the plastic ones always end up missin' before the next day rolls around. Some folks just ain't got no respect for the dead.

Love, Kisses, and Trailer Park Wishes,
Ruby Ann Boxcar

Chapter 9

# How to Do Gardenin' Without Breakin' a Sweat

*Dottie Lamb of Lot #14 shows just how simple it is to create a cornucopia of beauty in your yard with a few broken down TVs, a turntable hi-fi, some plastic flowers and plastic vines, and a hot glue gun.*

All right, I'll admit it! This chapter's title is a lie. Since most of our gardenin' takes place in late spring and throughout the summer, if you're at all like me, you can just look out your window durin' this time of year and start perspirin'. I guess what this section should actually be called is "Gardenin' Without Much Effort," but sure as I put that at the top of this chapter, I'd have people on me like dirt in your carpet. So I went with the better soundin' one. But, folks, the truth of the matter is that if you look at me you can clearly see that the last thing in the world I want to do is move a whole lot out in the sun. With that said, I got to tell you that I also don't want my yard to look like I don't care about how I live. So what me and my fellow residents at the High Chaparral Trailer Park have done is come up with a way for you to create a beautiful yard without havin' to work too hard at it. There are some real simple things that you can do without havin' to break your back, and I'm gonna share those tips with you.

When someone stops by to pay you a friendly visit, the first thing that they'll notice as they approach your trailer home is motor oil spots on your driveway. Well, they'll just have to get used to that 'cause that's natural and you ain't got time to be tryin' to clean that up. The second thing they'll notice before climbin' up those stacked-up cinder blocks to the rickety old wooden steps to your front door is your yard. Since most of us trailer dwellers rent our lots and don't actually own the grass that trailer sets on, why would we want to pay to have a new lawn put down even if the old one looks like a twister came through? And with all the dogs that wander around the parks, you'll never be able to get those burnt spots out of your yard, unless of course you put up a sturdy fence, which you'll have to take right down if you ever move or, Lord forbid, have to vacate the lot in the middle of the night. So forget about the grass portion of your yard. Your guests can just get used to the absence of grass. This means that the third thing they'll notice are the little yard statues and assorted decorations that beautifully litter your yard, but we'll get into to those later on in Chapter 10. So then, what is the final thing that actually impresses your guests before they step into your humble abode? Yes, that's right, it's your garden/outdoor floral arrangin' that will finally show your guests just how much you really care.

Now, these outdoor sections are different from anything we've done or will do indoors simply because when it comes to the outside we almost always use real flowers or plants. And since we got them darn kids runnin' through our yards along with stray dogs and wild creatures, we also put our garden/flowers in sections that they can't easily knock over or run though. So, put on those work gloves and get a hoe (no, you can't borrow my sister or Faye Faye, you got to do it yourself) and let's get to gardenin'.

## Washin' Machine Flowertopia

For our first project, we're gonna take an old run-down piece of machinery and turn it into a thing of beauty, which is kind of what we do with Me-Ma when we have our yearly family portrait taken in September. Since most of us have some kind of junk in our yards, like an old upright washin' machine, dryer, deep freeze, TV, or vacuum cleaner, it'd only make sense to use one of these eyesores when it comes to fixin' up our yards. Even though any one of these could easily be turned into a planter, I've decided to go with the easiest one, the washin' machine. Before we go any further, we have to decide what we want to put in it. Earlier I said that we almost always use real flowers in gardenin', but this is one of those times when we don't have to. Seein' how big that washin' machine is, we would need to shovel a lot of dirt inside it in order to plant the seeds for the flowers, which brings us to a very important question. Is that too much work? Some of y'all will say no, and will go for a week puttin' in two or three shovels' worth of dirt in it each day. And others of you will say yes. So since we got two options to consider, I guess we should look at the pros and cons.

The cons of goin' with the real flowers is that you've got to put them bricks in the washer first and then top 'em with your dirt and all. The pros is that you and your guests will be able to enjoy the wonderful aroma that comes from live flowers.

The cons for goin' with plastic flowers is that you won't get that wonderful smell. The pros are that you'll have flowers in your yard all year long.

Now that we've weighed both sides and you've made up your mind, I'm gonna show you how to do both methods. Ain't that easy? OK, let's get our hands a little dirty by startin' off with the real-flower method.

**SUPPLIES**

Old upright washin' machine
Drill
18 to 20 regular bricks
Shovel
Big bag of gardenin' dirt
Small to medium bag of milled peat, perlite, or a vermiculite mixture
Small bag of time-release fertilizer
Small bag of polymer
Flowers of your choice, seeds or seedlin's
Water

**1.** The first thing you're gonna want to do is have somebody in your trailer park who knows what he's doin' to come over and take the agitator out of that washin' machine. This should not be a big deal. After all, most the menfolk in my trailer park have no problems takin' apart either small or large pieces of machinery. It's puttin' 'em back together so they work that seems to be the issue with these fellas, which is why we got all them broken appliances and cars scattered all over the park.

**2.** Next you'll want to drill about 10 to 12 holes scattered along the very bottom of the washer. These holes will allow both water and air to flow through your plants and soil, which makes 'em go into some kind of process that's called capillarity (I have no idea as to what in the heck that is exactly, so please don't even stop me in the street if you see me to ask, 'cause I'll just look at you like you was loco or somethin'). Just make sure that your holes go all the way through the bottom since this is how the water and air drain out. You can check this by stickin' your head inside the tub and lookin' through the hole for light. If you can see light, you done good. If not, well, drill some more holes, hon.

**3.** We're gonna go ahead and put our bricks in the tub. The reason we're doin' this is so that we don't have to put a whole bunch of dirt in there. Go ahead and put seven bricks inside kind of like I pictured in the followin' graphic. Make sure that you don't cover up all the holes that you already drilled. That would be just terrible, as well as down right stupid. Now lay down on top of the first layer of bricks in a crisscross type fashion the next six or seven bricks. After that, put the rest of the bricks in also in a crisscross pattern. If you want to add more bricks, go ahead, but make sure that you leave at least one foot of space between the top of the washer tub and the highest brick.

**4.** Take your shovel and add the gardenin' dirt. If you bought a bag or bags of this gardenin' dirt, and you got a little bit of muscle, you can also just put a bag onto your laid-out bricks, cut a hole in the bottom of the bag, and scatter that dirt out that way. Regardless of how you do it, don't knock over your bricks and don't worry if the holes in the bottom of your washer gets dirt in 'em. As a matter of fact, some of your dirt might even start to come out the bottom. If you want to slow that down a bit, put

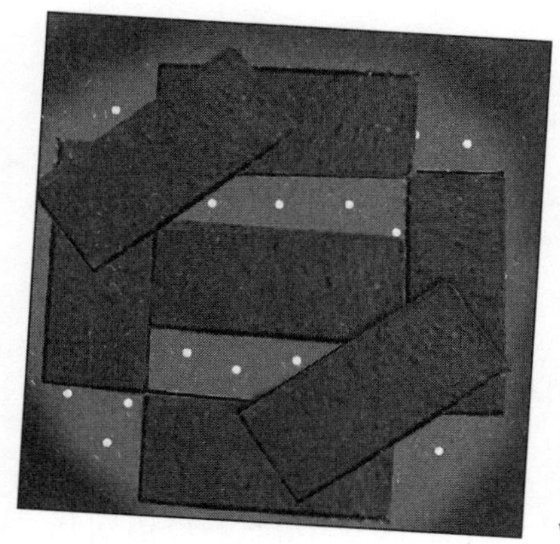

about an inch or two of dirt in first and then add a little water around the dirt where the holes are. This will help to form a little mud, which will stop the dry dirt from runnin' out. But personally I wouldn't worry about it all that much.

**5.** Put in 6 inches of the milled peat, perlite, or vermiculite mixture.

**6.** Add some of the time-release fertilizer and polymer and mix it in with the milled peat, perlite, or vermiculite mixture.

**7.** Top this off another 4 to 6 inches of the milled peat, perlite, or vermiculite mixture. Go ahead and add just a little more of that time-release fertilizer for good luck.

**8.** Add your flower seeds, or seedlins' to this new soil mixture. You can plant as many as you want, and since this is a trailer park, it don't matter if they match or not. Personally I like to put in all different kinds so that when one is not bloomin', the other ones are. Just ask the folks at the store where you buy your flowers which ones will work best for you. They know what goes best with the climate that you live in and which ones bloom when. Just remember to tell 'em what the lightin' conditions will be like (will there be lots of shade or not) so they can help to better serve you.

**9.** Add water. Typically you want to water your washin' machine until you see water comin' out the holes in the bottom. This will take some time 'cause of all the dirt, but be patient and keep the water comin'. The good news is that since you added that polymer like you did, it will hold a lot of water right there next to your flower roots so you only need to water twice a week (Sunday and Wednesday, Monday and Thursday, Tuesday and Friday, or whatever two days durin' the week work best for you). Just make sure that on those days you continue to add water until you see it flowin' or even just drippin' out of the bottom of the washin' machine. Oh, and even if it's been rainin' all week long, get out there and water them flowers on your waterin' day. Just know that it won't take as much water as usual to make your flowers happy.

**10.** The only thing else that you'll need to do is add some liquid fertilizer when the time-release stuff runs out. Read the directions on the bag and see how long they tell you it takes for the fertilizer to complete its work cycle (the expiration date ain't what you need, so keep readin'). When the cycle runs out, add new liquid fertilizer accordin' to the package instructions.

When it comes to our plastic-flower washin' machine version, it's still easy, with much less upkeep, but you'll still need to water it once a month. Well, maybe hosin' it down is a better way of puttin' it.

**SUPPLIES**

Old upright washin' machine
Drill
2 cinder blocks or 30 to 40 regular bricks
3 bricks
3 good-size pieces of dry floral foam
Regular roll of duct tape
Hot glue gun
Hot glue
Assorted plastic flowers

**1.** You're gonna need to get someone from around the park to get that agitator out of the washer. This should not be too hard to do.

**2.** Drill about 10 to 12 holes scattered along the very bottom of the washer. The last thing you're gonna want is a washer full of rainwater that's gone bad. These holes will make sure that if any moisture does get inside the washer, then it will run right out.

**3.** Put the two cinder blocks in the washin' machine. They should fit in sideways, but if you can't get 'em in the tub, then you're gonna have to switch over to them regular bricks. If that's the case, stack up them bricks like I showed you how to stack 'em in the real flower washin' machine directions, step number 3. The only difference from the way we laid the bricks there and the way we're gonna lay 'em here is that on this project we need them to stack all the way up to 6 inches from the top.

**4.** Take a piece of dry floral foam and set it on top of one of the 3 bricks. Take the duct tape and wrap it around both the left end of the foam and brick. Do the same to the right ends until the foam and brick are together. Repeat this for the remainin' 2 foams and bricks. The reason we do this is 'cause our foam and our flowers are very light and will easily blow away in high winds. So we got to weigh 'em down. It's the same type of theory that goes into why we put spare tires on the tops of our trailers. Once you got your foam bricks made, set 'em in the washin' machine.

**5.** Our last step is to stick the stems of our plastic flowers into the floral foam, but before we do this, we want to help make our arrangement last longer, so we will give the stems a real good shot of hot glue. Once you got that hot glue on a stem, push it right down in to the floral foam. You shouldn't have to hold it in place, unless it's a real windy day, and if that's the case, take your plastic flowers, hot glue gun and sticks, and floral foam bricks inside. You can put the artificial flowers into the foam right there on your kitchen table if need be. Then just take one planted foam brick at a time out to the washin' machine and stick it in there.

**6.** Last but not least, if a real bad storm is forecasted, don't hesitate to go out there and force that lid closed to save your babies. Just remember that the dears are fake and can be reshaped and bent to look just like new at a later date.

## Outdoor Sectionals

I love these projects 'cause not only do they always turn out lookin' so good, but me and my husband, Dew, can work on 'em together. I don't know if I just love doin' these kinds of things with him because we've been together for fourteen years come next August or if it's 'cause I can trick him into doin' most of the work. Whatever, a sectional can add a special touch to any yard, regardless if yours is made up of grass, blotches of grass, dirt, sand, or even just plain old concrete. So, let's get to work. I can't believe I used that ol' "w" word in a sentence like that.

**Supplies**

Tire
A few assorted cans of spray paint, any colors
8 rocks about the size of a golf ball
8 bricks
Small bag of sand
Piece of chicken wire, 2' x 2'
Big bag of regular gardenin' dirt
Shovel
Small bag of either milled peat, perlite, or a vermiculite mixture
Small bag of time-release fertilizer
Small bag of polymer
Flowers of your choice
Water

**1.** If you got a second car that you ain't usin', have your husband take one of the tires off and then have him take the tire itself off the rim. You ain't gonna hurt your tire at all. Or just get an extra tire from the top of your neighbor's trailer in the middle of the night.

**2.** Spray-paint that tire any festive color that you like. Most folks tend to go with red, white, and blue, but since this is a free country, pick your favorite. Set your tire aside and let it dry.

**3.** Pick a spot in your yard for your sectional.

**4.** Lay your tire where you want it. Take the rocks and place them on the ground right along the outside of the tire. Now, pick your tire back up and move each rock farther in so that the tire will rest on the rocks without 'em bein' seen.

**5.** Arrange the bricks on the ground inside the tire so that they're able to support the chicken wire as well as the weight of the dirt that you will eventually add. The reason we've put the rocks under the tire and the bricks on the ground on the inside of the tire is so that we can create a drainage without havin' to cut up the tire.

**6.** Go ahead and put sand in the inside rubber rim of the tire. Try to get it a little higher than the rim itself.

**7.** Place the chicken wire on top of this, allowin' it to rest on the bricks and bunchin' up on the insides of the tire.

**8.** Add ¼ to ½ the bag of gardenin' dirt with the shovel, or by simply pourin' it into the tire. Try makin' a crater in the dirt, pushin' some of it over to the sides of the tire.

**9.** Add ½ the bag of the milled peat, perlite, or vermiculite mixture.

**10.** Add some of the time-release fertilizer and polymer. Mix in with the peat, pelite, or vermiculite.

**11.** Add the rest of the bag of either milled peat, perlite, or vermiculite mixture.

**12.** Top off with some more of the fertilizer.

**13.** Plant your flowers.

**14.** Add water until you see it runnin' out from under the tire. Do this twice a week.

**15.** And enjoy!

See, you can have a lovely floral garden without havin' to break your back or doin' so much manual labor that they take away your certificate that states you're trailer trash. So have a good time and play around with what you already got. But most of all, do it for yourself and make your neighbors jealous.

## Ask Ruby Ann . . .

Dear Ruby Ann,

Since my septic tank has backed up into my neighbor's entire front yard, can I charge them a fee for fertilizin' their lawn and garden?

R.W.B
Baton Rouge, Louisiana

Dear R.W.B,

You scare the heck out of me, and I sure am glad I ain't livin' next to you. I can only imagine some of the stuff the poor folks who live in your trailer park must have to go through on a daily basis. Upon readin' your letter I quickly added them folks in Baton Rouge to my prayer list. And the answer to your question is yes.

Love, Kisses, and Trailer Park Wishes,
Ruby Ann Boxcar

# Chapter 10

# Yard Beautiful, the Trailer Park Way

*Ollie White of Lot #10 shows off her front yard display, and I got to tell y'all that it looks almost as good as it did before my mother in-law, Momma Ballzak, of Lot #16 accidentally drove her car through the display, reekin' havoc and carnage on Ollie's "little people."*

In the precedin' chapter I showed you how to make your yard a thing of beauty, and in this chapter, it's time to put the so-called icin' on the cake. We trailer dwellers do this by simply addin' decorations that we've either handcrafted or bought at a store or along the road. In some cases, we even use items that have been passed down from family member to family member for years. And then there are also those few items that the last person to reside on that trailer lot accidentally left when they hooked up their mobile home and fled in the middle of the night to avoid the sheriff or back rent payments. I know that some of y'all don't quite understand this whole concept on account of your upbringin', and so I'll try to explain it as best I can. If you look at your yard as bein' your face, then maybe this will all make more sense to you. For example, we've already put on our yard's base or foundation. Now all we have left to do is to simply apply its blue eye shadow, blush, and lipstick, if you will, before it can go out on the town. And nothin' does this as well as some yard statues, a few converted household and food containers, or one of them colorful wasp catchers.

In this chapter you are gonna learn how to craft a few of the always-popular-in-the-trailer-park decorative yet useful items from a few discarded materials that you've got lyin' around your yard already. And I'll also give you some of my time-tested secrets on how to keep those dang thugs from stealin' or vandalizin' your yard statues in the middle of the night. These really come in handy around Halloween, but I've found that if you use 'em on a regular basis, you don't have as much mess or bother when you get up on November 1. So grab your hot glue gun and your trash can 'cause it's time to decorate your yard in the High Chaparral Trailer Park tradition.

## A Trailer Park Birdbath

I just love animals, regardless of their size. That's why this trailer park birdbath is actually much more than the name alone would imply. Dependin' on how tall you make it and where you set it up, it can actually be a community drinkin' spot for all the wild animals that thirst for a refreshin' drink as they make their way through your yard. And another great thing about this yard-beautiful decoration is that it is so easy to put up and take down that you can relocate it to any part of your yard whenever you feel like it. Personally I like to set mine up so I can watch it from one of my windows while I enjoy a diet Coke or an RC Cola.

**Supplies**

3 tires
Spray paint
Large trash can lid, metal or plastic
Roll of duct tape

**1.** You can increase or decrease the actual number of tires that you use, dependin' on how short or tall you want your trailer park birdbath to be. I call for three, since that would be about average height, but please don't stick to that amount of tires if you don't want to.

**2.** Spray-paint the tires any solid or assorted colors that you want. Just remember that even though you can use every color in the rainbow, the last thing you want to do is create some bizarre color mix-match that is sure to frighten off even the most horrific bird that might be lookin' for a place to get a drink.

**3.** Pick a location for your birdbath and stack the tires up on top of each other right there.

**4.** Take your large trash can lid, the bigger the better, and inspect it for cracks or holes. Feel free to go over to the faucet and run a little water in it to help find any leaks. If you do happen to spot any, wipe that area dry and put a few pieces of duct tape on either side of the hole or crack.

**5.** Place the trash can lid with the handle side down on top of the tires.

**6.** Grab the water hose and fill up the lid. Every once in a while you might want to add a little fresh water when you see that the water is either gettin' low or turnin' unnatural colors.

## A Trailer Park Bird Feeder

Once again, just like with your birdbath, this feeder can also easily turn into a restaurant for all the animals that visit your yard, dependin'

on how tall you decide to make it. And just like with the birdbath, you can get hours and hours of fun and relaxin' entertainment by simply pullin' a chair up to the window as the wildlife stop by your wildlife truck stop.

**SUPPLIES**

3 tires
Spray paint
Large trash can lid, metal or plastic
Roll of duct tape

**1.** Again, build this one as big as you want. Personally I don't think I'd go down any lower than three tires since you ain't wantin' to feed all the animals that are in your trailer park.

**2.** I like to paint my feeder with the same colors that I used on my birdbath, but you can improvise on this approach and do whatever you want.

**3.** Pick a location close to your birdbath and stack the tires up on top of each other.

**4.** When it comes to holes or cracks on the trash can lid for the feeder, I just look for the big ones that will allow food to drop through. I touch up those openin's with duct tape.

**5.** Place the trash can lid with the handle side down on top of the tires.

**6.** Now you can throw birdseed or pieces of bread in the lid, or for that matter, old leftovers are always welcomed by our friends in the wild. Just keep an eye on what foods go fast and which ones are hardly touched. Even though the edible items are free, just like you have your own preferences, so do our wild friends. Make sure you dump out any water that might end up in the lid after a rain shower, and also dump out into a trash bag whatever might be left in the feeder every two days or so. Remember, just 'cause the neighbors might have rats don't mean that you need 'em too.

With your new lovely set of bird feeder and birdbath, your yard is sure to look just as nice and tasteful as anyone else's in the whole park. Yes, you're doin' your part to make your trailer community both beautiful and environmentally friendly. So give yourself a pat on the back, and throw some of them scraps out for the animals.

## Secrets of the Yard Statues

Nothin' will light up your yard like a lotful of them little statues. And even though they're only plastic or cement for the most part, the excitement they can bring is almost as fun as a Roman candle gone bad at a Fourth of July celebration. But the best part about these little folks is that unlike a plant or a rosebush, you ain't got to do nothin' to maintain 'em at their best. They're just there bringin' a smile to all who pass their way, givin' out a silent yell of "Hey, we're happy to be here!"

There are a few common-knowledge kinds of things that you newer trailer dwellers need to know about yard statues before you actually go out and bring some home. You might not know these unless you've spent most of your life in a trailer home. So, get that pencil and paper out and take a few quick notes.

- No self-respectin' trailer owner would ever think about puttin' a piece of wood in the yard that's painted to look like somethin' cute. I don't care if you got a jigsaw for Christmas and finally made somethin' with that old warped piece of plywood you've had lyin' up against the trailer since Carter was in office, don't paint it to look like it's somebody bent over pullin' weeds. Those one-dimensional pieces of crap are for those foundation-dwellin' trailer park wannabes. Please hear what I'm sayin' and leave the wood cutouts out of the yard.
- You can never have too many pink flamingos.
- Eight dwarfs is too many. If Snow White only needed seven to find a prince, then that should be just fine for your yard too.
- Bring your statues up to the front. Don't hide your poor little yard statues off in the back like they was that ugly child of yours that you lock in a closet with a bag of toys and a Fresca when company comes over. Show those lovely creatures off for all the world to enjoy.

Now that we got our basic rules down and out of the way, it's time for you to take a seat and brace yourself, 'cause the next part of keepin' a yard beautiful with lawn statues is a painful subject for many of us, but one that we can't just let go by without bringin' it up. And that subject is vandals. Oh, I break into a cold sweat and get weak-kneed just thinkin' about the damage a young hoodlum can cause to them little people who have only one job in life and that's to make everyone happy. But those juvenile degenerates don't care. They'll happily kick or push over anythin' concrete or plastic in your yard that's still got part of its head intact. And they don't care if you just bought it or it was a hand-me-down from your precious Pa-Pa. Them little thugs will beat it like it was a screamin' child at a Wal-Mart. That there is the gruesome fact, plain and simple. But the good news is that I've come up with a plan that I've been usin' for the past ten years, and I can proudly say that since I put it into action, not one of my little babies has been damaged, not even on Halloween. It's really simple, too. Yes, this plan of attack will give even those of you who'd given up on the chance of ever seein' another gnome in your yard again a new sense of hope. So here we go with the code name: Boxcar Bully Beater.

- Put a little cheap and easy-to-assemble fence up around your yard so that small children and animals can't get in. As you well know, this will not keep out the punks, but it will make sure that no person or animal is accidentally affected by our defense.
- Scatter bags of tacks around your yard in front of each lawn ornament. This won't stop everybody, but some of 'em will feel the sting.
- Take some 6-inch pieces of wood boards and drive several real long nails clean through each one. Follow this up by spray-paintin' the board and nails green if you got a lawn or tan if you ain't. Set these out in your yard. Just remember, the more the merrier, if you know what I mean.
- And last but not least, get yourself some of that hot wire/electric fence and hook it up to every one of your yard statues. Then you can run it directly under your trailer and hook it up to one of them high-powered electric fence chargers, and go to sleep. I promise that once you got your yard rigged with this baby, you ain't never gonna stay up at night worryin' about your yard statues again. And, dear reader, let me tell you, there ain't nothin' as comfortin' as wakin' up to the high-pitched scream of a juvenile delinquent with 240 volts runnin' through his body.

Now you ain't got no reason not to have a beautiful yard. And with these tips I've given you in this chapter, you're sure to have neighbors and even strangers drive by your place a little slower just to enjoy the view that you've created. And as you will soon learn, a happy yard makes for a happy life.

## Ask Ruby Ann . . .

Dear Ruby Ann,

I really would like a water fountain out in my yard, but all the ones on the market that I've seen just seem so gaudy to me. I don't want it to have children or angels or animals on it, but at the same time I don't want it to be to overly simple and plain. Do you have any suggestions?

Mike
DC

Dear Mike,

Oh, hon, don't I know what you mean! We had the same problem when it came to gettin' one for my daddy for his birthday this year. We knew he loved water and found a nice fountain to be both soothin' as well as inspirational. But we couldn't find nothin' we thought fit his personality. Everything seemed so womanlike as well. Finally after watchin' that Charlie gal on that English gardenin' show called *Ground Force,* I was inspired to take somethin' simple and rig it up to make the ideal waterworks for Daddy. Well long story short, when Daddy got back home from havin' dinner at the Sizzler, you should have seen his face. That toilet with the shootin' stream comin' straight out of the bowl that we put in his front yard, not only surprised him, but for the first time in my life, I saw my daddy cry. So take somethin' simple like that and create your own fountain of beauty.

Love, Kisses, and Trailer Park Wishes,
Ruby Ann Boxcar

# Chapter 11

# Money Matters

*They say money makes the world go round, and pictured here is the exact amount of money, usin' single $100 bills, it takes to go around my waist.*

Most of us here at the High Chaparral Trailer Park ain't got them 401(K) things, and from what I hear, those who do ain't got much of one left by now. In the past, us trailer park people have always pretty much been the kind of folks who liked to just keep it in the bank. We enjoyed the old tried-and-true money method of writin' checks. As a matter of fact, some of us had been known to write a check even when we didn't have any money in the bank, but I'm not here to talk about Little Linda. Yes, a checkin' account has always been just fine by us, but with the popularity of today's trailer park, things are changin'. These changes include the monetary worth of your neighbors and my neighbors as well. I mean, Dottie Lamb and Ben Beaver over in Lot #14, as well as Kenny and Donny in Lot #15, and Opal Lamb-Inman and Dick Inman at Lot #1 just got these new fancy debit Visa cards that take the money right out of your checkin' account. My niece, Lulu Bell, in Lot #8 and the Bunches over in Lot #3 have informed me that theirs are in the mail and on the way. Why, soon my sister, Donna Sue, who already has her paycheck directly deposited into her bank account, won't have to try to legibly write a check. Heck, she'll just be able to walk into Beaver Liquor and Wines, load up her shoppin' cart, and tell Ben to "swipe me, sweetie." And when it comes to credit cards, they're all over the place, and I ain't just talkin' about the ones from Fingerhut neither. Even Vance Pool in Lot #19 has a doggone MasterCard, secured of course. I tell you, there are people livin' at the High Chaparral Trailer Park who own more than one credit card, ain't over their limit, and, believe it or not, actually have their own names on 'em! I'm tellin' y'all, times have changed, which is why I can't see doin' a book on the life of trailer folks without talkin' about their money.

Regardless if you've just won the lottery in a state that don't consider it to be the Devil's Digits, or if you've recently pawned off all your ex's things and have a little extra money, you might be thinkin' about what to do with that new cash windfall. Some folks will tell you to put it in the bank, while others, like Sister Bertha of Lot #12, who still thinks an ATM card is the mark of the beast, will tell you to bury it under your trailer. But lately I've heard folks who are wiser than me suggest that while the stocks are still lower than they were back in the 1990s, it's a good time to invest in the market. Their theory is that in the long run the market will go up again, so buy while it's low and then sell when it's high. That makes sense, but you also have to consider that the market could drop even lower. It's just like gamblin' at one of them Indian casinos, except you're likely to be a winner since the stock prices in the past have always rebounded back eventually and you can't get brand-name cigarettes for $10 a carton. So say you decide to take a risk with that extra money that you now have, and you totally understand that playin' the market is a long-term endeavor. Which stocks do you invest in? Well, dear reader, that's a good question that I think I got the answer to. Even though I ain't got no money in the market at this time, I think that if I was goin' to put some in, I'd go with my own personal theory, which is real simple and easy. I call it Ruby Ann's Trailer Market Buyout. You get shares in the companies that make or sell products that trailer dwellers buy! Why? Because even if the economy drops like my big behind in a recliner and everyone in the High Chaparral has to go on welfare, we'll still be buyin' things that we don't need, but this time with the government's money. That's right, regardless of how bad the economy is, we folks will still be shoppin' like it's 1995. So with that in mind, I got an idea of which stocks would be the best to purchase, so get out that highlighter or take some more notes.

Now before I get started, I do want to make somethin' perfectly clear. Even though my neighbors call me the Suze Orman of the double-wide world on account of my suggestion that they put a dollar a week into a separate savin's account in order to save up for Christmas, I got to tell you that I'm by no means no kind of professional money manager. With the way I like to shop, if my books hadn't done so well, me and my husband would probably be bunkin' in at my sister's trailer and livin' off of what she makes as an exotic dancer. Lord, we'd have probably starved to death by now. So please take my remarks as ideas only and not as somethin' that Lou Dobbs or even them folks over at CNBC have recently discussed on either of their stations. If you like 'em, well, good, take 'em to your financial adviser and see what she or he has to say about 'em. I just want y'all to understand that I don't know how well these stocks have done in the past or, for that matter, how well they'll do in the future. I honestly have no idea whatsoever whether these mentioned stocks will go up or down tomorrow. After all, I ain't Martha Stewart. With that all said, here are my picks.

## Kraft

Hey, they make Velveeta, Tang, Kool-Aid, Easy Cheese, Jell-O, and other fine foods that we all eat and enjoy.

## Wal-Mart

How can an Arkansas-based store that sells the Kathie Lee Gifford line of clothin' go wrong?

## Any Beer Company

Just look in your neighbor's trash can and you'll see how that investment could turn out to be a big revenue return.

## WWE

(Formally known as the WWF)

If I got a dime for every time someone in the trailer park watched one of those pay-per-view wrestlin' events that they put on instead of payin' their phone bill or other utility statement, I'd be usin' a solid gold soaker tub to relax my tired achin' feet in.

## Cadbury Schweppes

Now I know that I've just thrown some of y'all for a loop with this stock pick, but hear me out. Yes this is a company from England, but have you ever tried one of them rich and gooey Cadbury Eggs that come out at Easter time? Oh, man, they'll put you into a two-week sugar shock! But them tasty little treats ain't the only reason that I suggest this company. No, I've picked Cadbury Scheweppes on account of the fact that they purchased a little Texas-based company back in 1995, which made them the proud owners of two lines of drinks that're known in trailer parks all over the world as the "juices of the gods." That's right, they own both Dr Pepper and RC Cola! And if that ain't enough, they also got A&W and Sunkist soda pops to add to their line of products. These folks might be from across the pond, but trust me when I tell you that somebody callin' the shots in this company has got trailer park blood runnin' through his veins!

## Smuckers

Not only do they make Goober, everybody's favorite peanut-butter-and-jelly combo in a jar, but they also own Crisco. Just like Loretta used to say, Crisco will do you proud every time.

## Dial

Yes, you done heard me right when I suggested that you add the Dial Corporation to your portfolio, whatever the heck that is. But why a soap company? Well, I got one word for you . . . Armour. That's right, the folks who produce such wonderful products like Renuzit air fresheners, 20 Mule Team borax, and Coast soap are also the same folks who own Armour Foods, which produce everyone's favorites Vienna Sausages (all seven flavors) and both the roast beef and corned beef hash. And with other fine food items like their chopped ham in a can, beef stew, and the entire Lunch Bucket selections, you can't go wrong with this one, either.

## Hormel

I can give you one word that will make you buy this stock . . . Spam. That's right, these folks can proudly claim the meat of the gods, Spam, as one of their many products that we trailer folks thoroughly relish.

## Fleming Companies, Inc.

Not only is Fleming one of the nation's largest food wholesalers who put out such great quality brands as Best Yet, Nature's Finest, and

Exceptional Value, but it also owns one of my all-time-favorite grocery store franchisers, Piggly Wiggly. Just remember, with Mr. Pig, you can't go wrong.

So good luck to y'all if you decide to invest, and I got this funny feelin' that one of these here stocks is bound to take you to Easy Street. Why if you get lucky enough, you just might be able to be like me and add a second story to your trailer home.

## Ask Ruby Ann . . .

Dear Big Hair Diva Goddess,

So can I buy stock in Gold Bond Medicated Powder? That stuff rocks in this Texas heat. Or how about Aqua Net? Are they on the stock market as well?

Randall P.
Austin, Texas

Dear Randall P.,

Let me start off with the Aqua Net question first. Amazin'ly enough the makers of this fine product, Chesebrough-Ponds USA Co., as far as I know are not listed on the tickertape. I know I use their product every day as do all the women and even the men, who still got some hair, at the High Chaparral Trailer Park. I just can't understand why they don't give us and the rest of the public a chance to show our undyin' support for all of their beautifyin' enterprise.

I got bad news as well when it comes to Gold Bond. They ain't on the market either. Lord knows if you had a piece of that, you and the rest of the stock owners would be livin' on Easy Street 'cause of my thighs alone. Oh, I go through that stuff like it was candy. And you can bet I take it with me everywhere I go. Why, I keep a bottle in the glove boxes of both our cars as well as one of them giant-size containers in the trunks. After all, you never know when you might need a refreshin' burst of Gold Bond Medicated Powder. Not only does it stop the chaffin', but after a dustin' of that tinglin' hard-workin' medicated powder, I could dance the rumba all night long, if I was a dancin' person. Yes, Randall, I, too, would have to give Gold Bond two thumbs up. Too bad we can't support this fine product any other way but bottle by bottle, or in my trailer home, case by case.

Love, Kisses, and Trailer Park Wishes,
Ruby Ann Boxcar

Chapter 12

# On the Road Travel Tips

*When it comes to road trips, nobody is as prepared as my sister Donna Sue of Lot #6, and nothin' is as equipped as her Bonneville. Of course you got to be real watchful on them sharp turns and especially careful on sudden stops, regardless if the top is up or down.*

With the success of my three previous books and the notoriety of Donna Sue's guide to bartendin' and so much else, I've found myself out on the road more often than one of my sister's trash-collectin', orange-jumpsuit-wearin' former boyfriends. Of course since I've been entertainin' folks as a temptress of song for now over twenty years, travelin' ain't really anythin' new to me, but I got to admit that it sure ain't the carefree come-and-go-as-you-will travelin' that I used to know. I've still got some tips that most folks who don't travel on a regular basis wouldn't know that might save 'em a little time and even money. For example, hardly anybody knows that your chances of bein' strip-searched at an airport are actually higher if you've got a metal plate in your head. Why, if airlines like United had made that fact public, I'm sure more trailer park dwellers would've taken to the skies a heck of a lot sooner as well as more often. And who'd have ever thought you'd need anythin' other than your driver's license to go from the U.S. to Canada and back? Nowadays, you got to show either a passport or an original or certified copy of your birth certificate and photo identification if you plan on visitin' our neighbors in the Great White North. And you can also forget about them bygone days when you and your buddies would jump in your car and drive down to Mexico for a good time with only your driver's license. Try that now and they'll send your butt back home, unless you're also carryin' a tourist card issued by a Mexican consulate or most of the airlines serving Mexico. Mind you, I ain't no travel agent or even that travel guru Peter Greenberg that I just love, but I am a gal whose had to get her and her sister's big behinds from place to place several times a year. Trust me, when it comes to travel, I know what I'm talkin' about. So, pack your bags and let's go.

## Ruby Ann's 100-Percent-Guaranteed Travel Tips

- *Never drive anywhere that ain't walkin' distance from your trailer in your own car.* Listen to me now when I say that I don't care how many hours you've spent on rebuildin' that engine or even tunin' the dang thing up, don't use it for travel purposes. You know as well as I do that if you drive your car for twenty to thirty minutes straight, it's gonna break down, and you're gonna be standin' outside that smokin' piece of junk waitin' for AAA (either your cousin Amos, Al, or Andy).
- *I don't care how far under the E that little arrow can get, get some gas.* Unless you can pee unleaded, get gas when your gauge says you've got less than a quarter of a tank. The last thing I want to do with my precious vacation time is set around in a hot car 'cause you think you got psychic abilities and can mentally project your mind into that gas tank. Just pull over and fill it up.
- *When you're almost out of gas, don't search for the best price.* I love to bargain-shop for groceries, but when I get to the point where I've got to eat or I'll pass out, I don't look at the prices. The same is true for gas. "But if I drive a little farther down the road I might find a better gas price." And if we run out of gas my can of mace might come out of my purse and spray your head off. Just pull over and get the gas.
- *When I tell you I need to stop for the bathroom, stop.* This is not a suggestion or even a hint. And unlike that "world's largest dirt dauber nest" that you said you wouldn't mind stoppin' at, this stop I'm talkin' about is a must. So unless you got flood insurance on your automobile, pull the dang car over now.
- *A ditch along the highway is not the same as a ladies' room at the Stuckeys.* That's like sayin' a can of tuna is the same as a dinner at Red Lobster. I got a feelin' if you had to do your business while duckin' and dodgin' wild animals and the headlights of semi-trucks, it'd be a whole 'nother ball game.
- *Weigh stations mean business.* The last time I stopped at one of

them stations I had to leave my watch and a knee-high before they let me go on.

- *The only thing worse than havin' to use a bathroom on a bus is gettin' a seat next to it.* I don't care if you have to swap out your sister for a seat closer to the front, do it. You'll be mighty glad.
- *If you take food on a bus, make sure you got plenty for everyone.* Just trust me on this.
- *Even the most unattractive airline employees can get free air travel for people they date.* Hey, it could be worse. You could be datin' a bus driver. So close your eyes and kiss him, Momma needs a trip to Vegas.
- *When flyin' always bring a spare outfit in your carry-on.* If you're my size and they misplace your luggage for a few days, the only way you're gonna be able to wear the largest-size slacks or dress that they got at the local Banana Republic or Express is if you wear it as a scarf.
- *All cruise ships have pools that guests can swim in.* So don't forget to pack your cut-off jeans. With that said, I hate to tell you that water-skiin' off the back of the boat ain't gonna happen.
- *Call the front desk if you find a bug in your room.* I don't care what the motel's policy is, if I find a bug in my room, he's payin' half the bill.
- *It's cheaper to fly freight.* Who said Me-Ma can't come with us to New York?

## Ask Ruby Ann . . .

Dear Ruby Ann,

Since I'm single, I always take my eighty-four-year-old neighbor with me when I go on vacation. Usually I pick the place and since I'm paying for it, I take her along. Well, the dear has really had a bad year and her hearing and vision aren't what they used to be. Healthwise she is fine and can keep up with me easily. But since I knew that her sight would make or break this year's trip I wanted to do something special for her, so I asked where she wanted to go. She said she wanted to see the stars in Branson. Well, Branson is great for an eighty-four-year-old woman. But since I like to drink and I smoke,

Branson isn't going to be a thrill ride for me. I'd much rather go gambling. What should I do?

Kristi
Oklahoma City, Oklahoma

Dear Kristi,

Your problem is easily solved. Go to Vegas and tell her it's Branson. With her vision problem she'll never know. And as far as the stars go, drop her off at one of them impersonation shows. By the time she goes home, she'll think she's seen all the big names in show business, and she'll swear that Judy Garland is still alive. Just make sure you get back in time to pick her up, 'cause at some of them places when the show's over they push the stragglers out into the street. And if she says anything about all the bright colors at night, just tell her it's on account of a full moon and them crazy Northern Lights. What the heck, she ain't gonna know.

Love, Kisses, and Trailer Park Wishes,
Ruby Ann Boxcar

# Chapter 13

# Overnight Guests: Strangers in the Night

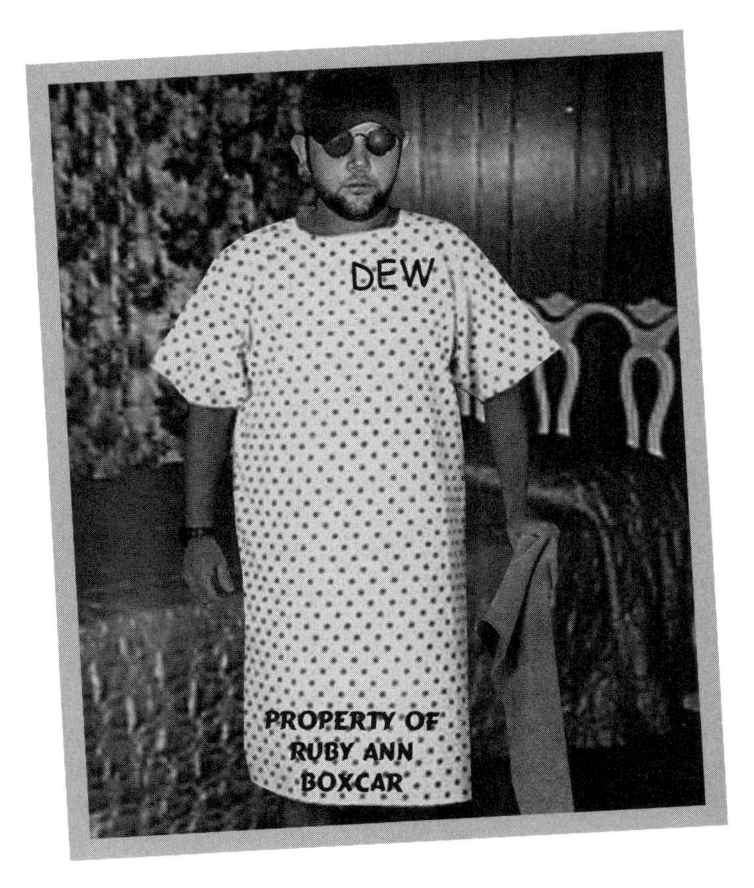


*My husband, Dew, who shares Lot #18 with me, steps out of the shower and into his new pajamas, which I made for him out of a hospital gown for Christmas. As you can clearly see, he's just thrilled as can be with his present.*

I don't know about y'all, but if there is one thing I hate to do, it has to be stayin' overnight at someone's home. I don't care how nice that person is or how close we are, I just don't like it. I guess it's on account of the fact that I like to be me at night after my host and hostess have gone to bed. If I want to walk to the fridge to get a late-night snack with nothin' on but the toilet paper I've got wrapped around my hair to protect its bouffantness, then so be it. Or if I want to stay up a little longer to watch TV, I don't want to worry about disturbin' the kind folks who've opened up their home to me regardless if it's on wheels or not. Call me weird, but that's the way I am. I'd much rather check into a motel or hotel than feel uncomfortable in another person's home. Why, back when we had them plumbin' problems and my toilet exploded a few years ago on Christmas Eve night, forcin' me and my husband, Dew, to have to stay with Momma and Daddy, I felt uneasy the entire time. I mean, so what if I'd bought them that trailer home as well as practically everything else they got inside it with the hard-earned money I work like a dog to make. I still felt weird stayin' with 'em for even that one night. And although the visit went without a hitch, I can promise you that if my toilet ever explodes again and all the motel rooms are full in Searcy or up at Tina Faye's R.U. Inn, I'm drivin' to Little Rock if that's what it takes to rent a room for the night. But don't get me wrong, I'll stay at your house from the time you're awake until you're ready to hit the hay, but the times before or after I don't want to be anywhere near the place.

Since I know that I ain't the only person out there that feels that way, and that others ain't as blessed financially as me to be able to afford the cost of a motel room, I've come up with a way to make your guests feel at ease as well as just as relaxed as they would if they was payin' $25 a night. These surefire tips will make your guests happy and content and even able to sleep soundly all night long without the worry of bein' a bother. So go ahead and get out that address book and call all those friends that you've wanted to have come visit you from out of town, and then let's get to turnin' that spare bedroom and bathroom into a Motel 6 experience.

## Personalized Soap

I'm real weird when it comes to my bath soap. I don't like to use a bar of soap that someone else has used already unless of course it happens to be my husband, Dew. But even then I got to lather it up real good and then rinse it off. So you can imagine my horror when I get to a place where I have to bathe and the soap is lyin' there open. I just wash with my shampoo when that happens. And I know that my own houseguests must feel the same way that I do, which is why I've come up with somethin' that will make both me and my guests happy. Since I hated buyin' new soap for a guest only to end up throwin' it away as soon as they leave 'cause I wouldn't dream of touchin' that bar to my skin after they've had it on their body parts, I decided to simply transform that soap as well as all the little ones that I got stacked up in my shower. Just wait till you try this one.

**SUPPLIES**

Slivers of soap
Bar of soap
1 tablespoon water
Sardine can

**1.** Take all them slivers of soap and that bar that your guest used while they was there, and cut 'em up into little pieces. Put 'em in a bowl and add the water.

**2.** Put in a microwave and cook on high for 3 minutes. Stir and add extra water if you need. Nuke it for 2 more minutes. Stir.

**3.** Pour the contents into the sardine can and allow it to cool and harden.

**4.** Take a knife to loosen it up, and pop it out.

**5.** Take one of them empty soap boxes that you saved from your last motel visits, the ones that had your hotel soap in it, and put your new soap in that.

**6.** Superglue the package shut, and place it in your guest bathroom.

## Bed Sheets

I keep busy entertainin' all the guests that stop by my trailer every month. It seems like one person will leave and another one comes in just hours later. Even though I want all my visitors to feel special, I just ain't got that kind of time it takes to change the sheets, throw 'em in the washer, put on a fresh pair, and take care of all the other activities I got goin' on in my daily life. So I've come up with what I think is a great way to handle this little hospitality problem.

**1.** When your last guest says good-bye and walks out the trailer door, go to the guest bedroom that they was in and pull down the bedspread.

**2.** With one hand, lift up the top sheet while usin' the other to quickly run your Dustbuster over the bedsheet. You ain't got to cover that whole sheet, just give it a quick once-over.

**3.** Repeat this process from the other side of the bed. Now lift up the top sheet once again and take your disinfectant spray and give it a quick blast down between the sheets. Give the pillows a quick spray while you're at it.

**4.** Make the bed and move on with your life.

Folks, don't get me wrong with this bed thing. Yes, you should eventually wash them guest sheets, but once every two or three months is enough. You ain't runnin' a boardin' house or nothin'. If your guests want spankin' clean linen, then they can go get a hotel room.

## Guest Pajamas

You know, I like to make my trailer houseguests feel special, so I always make sure to do little things like place a piece of candy that was leftover from last year's holiday season on their pillow at night, provide them with a spare toothbrush that one of my sister's many ex-boyfriends left unclaimed at her trailer, and even have pajamas with their names on 'em for them to wear at night when they go to bed. I know it sounds like I go all out, but really, it's pretty simple. Take the pajamas for example. All I do is take an old hospital gown and write their name on it in felt-tip marker. Of course, I learned that if you only put their first name, like, say, Bob, on the front, then you can reuse it each time someone named Bob or Robert shows up to stay the night. Just whatever you do, don't get it wet 'cause sometimes that marker will run all over the place. Just give it a light shot of your favorite air freshener after each Bob leaves. And of course, your guests will be glad you took the time to make them feel like they mean the world to you.

## Ask Ruby Ann . . .

Dear Ruby Ann,

What is the proper and polite thing to do when you see unwanted houseguests pull up and get out of their car? I don't want to be rude, but what can I do about these people who forget that you have a life of your own to live, and might even have already had plans.

Howard
Boston, Massachusetts

Dear Howard,

I got problems with them kinds of folks, too, which is why I always keep a QUARANTINE sign, which I swiped off of my sister, Donna Sue's trailer a few years back, right next to my front door. I just let the sign do the talkin', and I ain't had to change my plans in years on account of uninvited guests.

Love, Kisses, and Trailer Park Wishes,
Ruby Ann Boxcar

# Chapter 14

# Paintin' the Town

*Pastor Ida May Bee and husband, Brother Woody Bee, of Lot #7, shown here leavin' one of their favorite Sunday after-church buffets, believe in gettin' what you pay for at a restaurant, just like the rest of us at the High Chaparral Trailer Park.*

Now, don't y'all worry, 'cause when I use the word, "paintin'" I ain't suggestin' that you do any kind of manual labor. What kind of a gal do you think I am? I'm simply referrin' to the old sayin' about "paintin' the town red," which basically means to go out for a night of fun. You know, like maybe havin' dinner at the Sizzler, Golden Coral, or Furr's Cafeteria, and then catchin' a movie over at the Dusty Comet Auto Park Drive-In. Or it could be as simple as dinner at the Taco Tackle Shack followed by a go on the mike at Anita's Bar and Grill durin' karaoke night. For that matter, I can't tell you how many times me and my husband, Dew, have made a night of it by havin' a bite up at the concession stand in between frames of a heated bowlin' game at the Great Big Balls Bowling Alley. The point is that you can paint the town red for next to nothin', but you can't do it by simply settin' around your trailer home watchin' reruns of *The Andy Griffith Show* while your dogs give you a relaxin' yet therapeutic foot massage with their tongues. You've got to get out of that trailer from time to time. Yes, dear reader, even King Arthur left his castle on occasion. But unfortunately many of us trailer dwellers don't know how to act properly when we do finally get our car to hold a start and head into town. And I blame this fact on the folks who manufacture trailers. If they didn't make 'em so doggone luxurious and fit 'em out with top-of-the-line furniture, maybe we might feel the need to leave our abodes once in a while. But oh no, with things like openin's big enough to fit the latest air conditioner window unit, almost-real-lookin' brick fireplaces with plastic logs that appear to glow red from the hidden fifteen-watt lightbulb below, simulated-rock trailer skirtin', and shag-carpeted floors that are now strong enough to support a couch containin' a 330-pound woman, a love seat with her much smaller husband, and a big-screen TV without bowin', sinkin', or just givin' straight in and droppin' right out, most of us have chosen to simply stay inside our homes and leave the world behind. Because of this, our on-the-town wisdom, just like the vision of them bats that live deep in underground caves, has atrophied from lack of use. Oh sure, we know how to act when we got company over or go to a neighbor's mobile home for a friendly game of Skip Bo, but as I've witnessed in recent years, we've lost that style, that flair, yes, that basic way of actin' in public that I think the French so beautifully refer to as *"ménage-è-trois."* Or maybe it's *"je ne sais quoi."* It's somethin' like that. Anyways, this chapter will focus on things to remember when you go out to eat. Now, this is not etiquette, as some folks would like to call it. I'm not tellin' you which fork to use or where to put your napkin or nothin' like you'd find in one of them thick etiquette books that you see in the library, but rather it's just some everyday common knowledge that you need to use when you and your people go out for a night on the town. So please make a mental note of these tips, or, for that matter, bring this book along with you, and do your *best,* so that you don't make us fellow trailer park folks look bad out in public.

## Goin' Out to Eat

Generally speakin' there are six different types of ways you can go and get food and five different kinds of places where this chow will be. Those places and types are:

- *Fancy restaurants.* These are where you actually sit at a table and have a waiter or waitress.
- *Self-serve restaurants.* These are when you actually sit at a table, but you place your order at the counter or over a phone and not with a waiter or waitress.
- *Drive-ins.* These are where you pull in to a parkin' spot, turn your car off, and place your order.
- *Drive-thrus.* These are where you don't park or shut your car off, but simply place your order and drive to the next window to get it.
- *Pickup or takeout from all of the above.* This is when you call your order in so you can pick it up and take it home.

- *Dinner theaters.* These are where you actually sit at a table and have a waiter or waitress who also happens to be a member of the cast that does a play or musical show right after dinner.

Now that we have established all six methods of dinin' that require folks to leave their home in order to get a cooked meal, let's take a look at each one individually. This is where you're gonna want to take your notes or get out your highlighter.

## Fancy Restaurants

*(Red Lobster, Denny's, Anita's Bar and Grill, Village Inn, the Pangburn Diner, Steak and Shake if you eat inside, and of course, the Blue Whale Strip Club, to name just a few)*

Let me start this section off by tellin' you to never, and I do mean *never,* take your silverware home with you. That's just plain old tacky and pure white trash. When your waiter comes to clear off the table before presentin' your check, he or she is goin' to notice if your silverware's missin'. How embarrassin' will that be when y'all have to pull the silverware out of your pockets and purses? Don't be stupid. Take the silverware from one of the empty tables for goodness' sake. Your waiter'll just think that the dang busboy or busgirl wasn't doin' his or her job as usual and light into the buser instead. After all, everyone knows that waitin' staff think the table busers are lazy, incompetent fools anyways. Chewin' 'em out for not puttin' silverware on a table when they bused it will be the highlight of that waiter's day. And in the long run, your swipin' another table's silverware will be a blessin' to the buspeople as well, 'cause after they've been read the riot act by the waiter, they'll get ticked off and start takin' even more of that waiter's tips from tables when they clean 'em. So the waiter joyously has a reason to yell at the busboy, the busboy makes more money that night, and you got a lovely new silverware settin' for four. When done right as I've just described, it's a win-win situation all around.

Condiments are a different matter. There are some that you can take right from your table, if done correctly, and some that you can't. Ketchup, mustard, steak sauce, and other sauces that they bring in a bottle to your table can be sneaked out without any problems. If anybody asks, just tell 'em that one of the employees came by and asked if y'all needed it anymore, then took it. Another thing you can do is put a little bit of what you're takin' home on your plate. Then, when your waiter is out of sight, grab a busboy that hopefully speaks English, and ask for a bottle of whatever you're heistin'. If he don't speak English, just point to that bit of sauce on your plate and make a gesture like you're pourin' somethin' out of a bottle. He'll understand what you're sayin', bring it on over, and now you'll have the condiment to leave on the table. Of course, feel free to switch out bottles if the second one's got more in it.

Salt and pepper are different, too, since they come in nice dispensers. In this instance you've got two choices. You can either try the busperson thing where you pocket the original set and get him or her to bring you a second one, which you leave on the table, or if you carry plastic sandwich bags with you, you can pour out the salt and pepper. I know when we Boxcars all go out to eat we attempt the first, especially if the shakers are different or fun-lookin', and if that don't seem to work, we switch over to the latter plan of action. Just remember to put the shakers in a plastic bag so they don't spill out into your purse or pocket.

Sugar, salt, and creamer packets are always welcomed in our pockets or purses, too. You can easily dump all the packets out and ask for more without anyone bein' the wiser. For all the waiter knows, the dang thorn in his side known as a busboy either forgot to refill the container or he picked up your empty used packets already. So when it comes to these condiments, you can never walk away with too many. And who's to say you didn't put creamer in the Dr Pepper or Orange Crush you're drinkin'?

Napkins are always needed around my trailer home, but let me just warn you now, leave the cloth ones behind. Y'all already got enough laundry to do. You don't need no dang cloth napkins to clean as well. But if they got paper napkins, stuff those babies neatly into your pants, under your hat, or down your bra! The more the better when it comes to these restaurant products. And the good thing is that waiters and waitress as well as busboys are always happy to bring you extra napkins by the handfuls with no questions asked. Heck, if a manager comes to my table and asks how everythin' is, I won't hesitate to ask for more paper napkins, after I've praised both the food and our waiter.

Regardless of what you might be drinkin', always ask for two lemon wedges. These can fit easily into any sandwich bag for later use when you're makin' lemon desserts or even lemon chicken. Just remember to ask for two each time you get a refill.

The answer to the question "What about the rolls of toilet paper in the bathrooms" depends on your sex. If you're a man, I'd say leave 'em be, or take just one and stuff it in the front of your pants. Of course this can delay your flight from dinner just a bit on account of women wantin' to give you their phone numbers. But trust me, gentlemen, don't call any woman like that, regardless of how attractive she might be, 'cause both you and her will quickly be highly disappointed in the long run. Now women, regardless of their size, can take all the toilet paper they want. They can put it in their purses, in their bras, as well as in the backs of their slacks as far as that goes. Heck, my niece, Lulu Bell, has been known to walk out of a restaurant with four rolls in her bra, six in the seat of her dress, two in her purse, and they was all double-ply. God bless her, she ain't got much upstairs, or downstairs in the rear either. Once my sister, Donna Sue, tried shovin' into her girdle a whole case full that she'd found under the sink at a Denny's while we was passin' through Sapulpa, Oklahoma. When we went up to the counter to pay, the toilet paper had moved around so much that the cashier asked her when the baby was due. Knowin' my sister had been hittin' one of the many flasks she carries with her at all times, I told the guy that it should arrive in two weeks, put my money on the counter, and commenced to leave. My sister on the other hand took this fella's question as a pickup line and started talkin' to him. When I realized what was goin' on, I rushed back and said that we had to go if we was goin' to meet the baby's father when he got done with his shift at the police station, and headed Donna Sue towards the door. Well, about that time, one of them rolls of toilet paper had miraculously managed to squeeze itself out of the tight bonds of my sister's girdle, and fell out of her dress and right onto the floor in front of the cash register. Without blinkin' an eye, I kicked it across the restaurant and under a table, turned towards my sister, and in a sharp voice I said, "I told you that you needed a bigger pad." Of course then we both hurried out the door and raced onto the highway.

While we're in the bathroom, when it comes to those disposable paper toilet seat covers, grab 'em up. Not only do they come in handy when visitin' an untidy neighbor's trailer for a night of cards, but they're also great for hair wraps. They easily fit over your hair and onto your forehead, which in turn allows you to use less toilet paper when you wrap your updo at night before goin' off to bed. Just make sure not to waste your time with those cheap paper towels that don't do nothin' but tear apart in your hands. Leave those where they are for the uneducated.

Now, I know that some of y'all who happen to be readin' all this might consider our actions as stealin'. Well, all I got to say to that is "shame on you for thinkin' that way." I'll have you know that all my family members are good Baptists who wouldn't give a thought to stealin', with the exception of my sister who has been known to steal a married man from time to time. And in her defense, she was drunk and had no idea what she was doin'. When it comes to eatin' out, we are only takin' what is rightfully ours. And after I say that I know there are still some of you who will insist that the price we pay at the end of the dinner is for the food only. Come on, do you really think that little old hamburger on two pieces of stale bread and a handful of fries could really cost $6.95? And I suppose that glass of pop that would cost you fifty cents at the corner vendin' machine really does cost the restaurant a whole dollar? No, they include the price of the condiments, napkins, and toilet paper in your check at the end of your dinin' experience. Why, my daddy will go into a restaurant bathroom, unroll some toilet paper, and toss it in the toilet unused just 'cause the cost was included in his bill. I've even known him to actually use the soap and wash his hands before rejoinin' us at the table if he thought the prices were a bit steep. Surely you don't think that the restaurant likes you so much that they're givin' that stuff to you for free? If that was the case, then they'd give you $6.95 worth of food in the first place. You pay for it, so you might as well use it.

As far as the bowlful of mints or other candies that you'll find on the counter by the cash register goes, these are complimentary and not included in the price of your bill. It would be morally wrong to take more than one unless an employee offers them to you. Let that employee have to account for his or her thievin' actions from that restaurant at the Pearly Gates, not you.

## Self-Serve Restaurants

*(McDonalds, Subway, Arby's, Taco Tackle Shack, KFC, White Castle, Dairy Queen, and Long John Silver's, to name just a few)*

You'll be hard pressed to find any bottled sauces or cloth napkins in any of these food joints. The reason for this is on account of them not incorporatin' that kind of crazy cost into your food bill. When you get a $4.00 meal, you're gettin' a lot more food for your money. But there are still some items that they include in this price that're just waitin' for you to come and pick up. The golden rule in these restaurants is that if it's bolted down, it ain't included in your bill.

Not only are the paper napkins screamin' your name, but let's be honest, who can't use an extra napkin holder? And the good thing is that they're just the right size for either your purse or one of those paper bags they serve your food in when you get it to go. So eat the food there and use the bag for the holder. Ain't they thoughtful?

How many times have you had someone over to your trailer that needed a straw? Well, thanks to these self-serve restaurants, your guests will never be strawless again.

Why be limited to just a bottle's worth when you can have all the ketchup, mustard, mayonnaise, relish, diced onions, and BBQ sauce that you want, thanks to those handy little packets? Just make sure to take 'em out of your back pockets before gettin' into your vehicle.

If they ain't got the toilet paper trapped behind some kind of metal contraption, feel free to export that as well. And while you're in there, get some more of those paper seat covers.

## Drive-Ins

*(Sonic, A&W, Del Rancho, and Coits, to name just a few)*

Obviously, in most cases, the bathroom pilferin' is pretty much out of the question at these places. Other items that you can mark off your list are napkin and straw holders, bottles of anythin', and silverware. You can also plan on not gettin' anythin' by the handfuls when you go to a drive-in. But don't let this get you down, 'cause there is one item that is included in your food cost, and that, dear reader, is known in the restaurant business as the "tray." Yes, that tray is our brass ring, if you will. Forget the glass mugs. Even though they might be nice, they are not included in your cost. Takin' those, just like with the complimentary mints, would be stealin', and you'd be sure to serve some time in either hell or the Republican Party for such an act.

The trays are easy to obtain, you just have to know how. Number one, never park in an area where the employees can look out the window and see you. That's just stupid. These drive-ins have tried to cater to your every need by brickin' in most of their restaurant. They really want you to be able to get the tray that you and your family deserve. Number two, don't take the tray and everythin' that's on it. You want to leave your trash on the counter or out by where your car was. This way, if someone should ask you about it, you can say, "Hey, the trash is there, so more than likely what happened was when I left, some thug must have dumped it before runnin' off with the tray." Now it ain't a lie when the property rightfully belongs to you. And every once in a while some of them thugs could use a good butt-whoppin' just to keep 'em in line. So not only in this case have you got your tray, but you've also done your civic duty when it comes to troubled teens.

## Drive-Thrus

*(Anita's Bar and Grill, Hardee's, and the Fisherman's Friend, to name just a few)*

Even though this way of gettin' your food is fast and convenient, it sucks when it comes to the price you pay versus what you get for your dollar. Normally the restaurants that offer drive-thru service charge the same prices regardless if you eat inside or pull through. But you got no control at all over how many napkins, condiments, or straws you can bring home with you. Oh sure, you can always ask for more, but don't count on reapin' the bounty you would've had if you'd been able to control the flow yourself. But sometimes you do get lucky and the guy or gal workin' the window is too busy to care, so you end up with a bag containin' handfuls of treasures. Of course, findin' an employee at a drive-thru who doesn't take pride in their work is next to impossible I'm sure. So I'd say if y'all ain't in a hurry, go inside for goodness sakes, and help yourself.

## Pickup or Takeout

*(Taco Tackle Shack, Daddy Lamb's Pizza, and Anita's Bar and Grill, to name just a few)*

Now this is basically just the same as the self-service style of dinin' except you got a quicker get-away. So see Self-serve Restaurants for details.

## Dinner Theaters

This, my friends, is where we separate the professionals from the amateurs—and I ain't talkin' about the actors up onstage. Since your waiter is also a member of the cast, he ain't got a lot of time to spend watchin' you and your table, so you could walk out of there with an entire table settin'. Not yours, of course, but you get the picture. Because this is so easy, lots of people who ain't been properly learned in this area will tend to go overboard and finger themselves out. There ain't no place for greed when it comes to dinin' out!

I'll never forget the time I went to the now defunct Pearls Before Swine Dinner Theater that was located just outside of Heber Springs. They'd taken an old pig farm and turned it into a theatrical palace, and once you got over the smell, it sure was somethin' to behold. I got to tell you their performance of *Grease* was one of the best I've ever seen, despite the fact that the youngest cast member had to be pushin' fifty-five, and the part of Frenchy was played by a pig in a wig and poodle skirt. Of course the pig didn't really sing or speak the part, the three-piece orchestra leader, Mr. Glenn Freed, did all that voice-over stuff offstage. Even though they had to throw an ear of corn on the area of the stage where they wanted Frenchy to stand, none of us found it distractin' from the performance at all. What we did find distractin' was this clink-clankin' sound that filled the theater durin' the big "Greased Lightning" number. It was almost like Tinkerbell was in the buildin'. Of course it didn't take long for the staff to figure out where the noise was comin' from. It was the table next to us. It seemed that they'd loaded themselves down with so much silverware, drinkin' glasses, and other assorted items that when they clapped and tapped their feet to the upbeat music, all their hidden goods collided together. Why, they'd gotten so into the show that they didn't even notice the sound they was puttin' off. Not only was it embarrassin' for these folks when management made 'em empty out their pockets and purses right in front of everyone before throwin' 'em out of the theater, but they missed Frenchy's tear-wrenchin' reaction to the scoldin' lyrics of "Beauty School Dropout." Poor amateurs. Like I said earlier, there ain't no place for greed when it comes to dinin' out.

Now that you know the secrets of dinin' out, you've got no reason to stay in, unless of course you happen to be poor. If that's the case, just treat yourself to a pretend dinner out right in your own dinin' room. Make it even more fun by takin' things from your own trailer home. In any case, enjoy.

## Ask Ruby Ann . . .

Dear Ruby Ann,

What is the appropriate amount you should tip a good waiter? My daddy swears the standard amount to leave is 10 percent. Is he right?

Beverly M.
Durant, OK

Dear Beverly M.,

Tippin' your waiter or waitress is very important. In most cases, they only make minimum wage, so they survive on your gratuity. Now if all your daddy has been leavin' is a 10 percent tip, the next time he visits his favorite restaurant, he might want to check his drink before indulgin' in it if you know what I mean. I've got to tell you that I've never heard of havin' a waiter do everything he or she can to make sure my meal is just like I ordered it and that I got plenty to drink for a 60¢ tip on a $6 tab. Heck, that won't even buy him a bottle of RC Cola. I'm sure the waitin' staff must hide when they see your cheap tightwad daddy walk in the door.

Way back when I was just a little girl, 15 percent of the bill was considered a good amount to tip, but that was when you could get a soda pop for 10¢. Nowadays, the standard most places is 20 percent. When you consider, as I mentioned above, all the hard work that these men and women do to make your dinin' experience a delight, I think that 20 percent is more than fair (presumin' the service was deservin' of reward). That means that when my bill is $6 I leave $1.20 for the waiter. If it's $25 my waiter will find a nice $5 bill on the table after I've left. And if the entire Boxcar clan gets out together for a meal, the waiter will usually get $20 since we eat right around $100 by the end of the meal. It's that simple.

Now I know that some of y'all out there may not have a 20 percent cash tip to leave your waiter, but yet you don't want to look cheap like Beverly's daddy neither. What can you do? Just leave as much of the tip as you can in cash, and then swap out the difference in food. Go ahead and leave 'em a few fries or onion rings next to the tip. A bite-size portion of your burger is at least worth 75¢. And can you really put a price on a chicken leg with a little meat left on it? Everybody loves a dinner roll, so thank your waiter by leavin' him or her what's left of that one you couldn't finish. If your waitperson happens to be lactose intolerant, he or she can easily scrape off that butter. And if the service was exceptionally good, leave a few sugar packets beside the rest of the tip to let your waiter know that the service went far beyond what you expected.

Love, Kisses, and Trailer Park Wishes,
Ruby Ann Boxcar

# Chapter 15

# Helpful Hints

*Some of the gals that call the High Chaparral Trailer Park home share helpful hints as well a prayer request with each other as they gather at Connie Kay's for a special demonstration on some product line that she handles. Of course seein' how we're good Baptists, we don't gossip at these gatherin's, but simply tell you all the details so when you pray for someone, you know what you're prayin' about. Standing, from left to right: Wanda Kay of Lot #13, Juanita Hix of Lot #9, Tina Stopenblotter of Lot #17, Momma Ballzak of Lot #16, Lois Bunch of Lot #3, Sister Bertha of Lot #12, Connie Kay of Lot #13, Lulu Bell of Lot #8, and Anita Biggon of Lot #2. Seated, from left to right, are Wendy Bottom of Lot #4, Kitty Chitwood of Lot #11, Nellie Tinkle of Lot #4, and Momma Boxcar of Lot #5.*

What would a Ruby Ann Boxcar book be without a few helpful hints from my neighbors at the High Chaparral Trailer Park? Well, it just wouldn't be the same, and I'd have some mad-as-all-get-out neighbors to boot. So I went door to door this go-round and told everyone that I was workin' on a trailer park lifestyle book and would be pickin' up any helpful hints they wanted to add on the followin' Sunday after church. Well, to be honest, after dinner was when I went out and picked these up, 'cause I knew that even with that deadline, some folks still wouldn't be ready till then. Sure enough, most of my neighbors had just finished gatherin' their hints together, while others had well over a thousand for me to put in this here book. God bless 'em, ever since that first book when I paid 'em a dime for each hint, they just keep makin' bigger and bigger lists. Of course I stopped payin' 'em with cash since then and now I just buy 'em all little gifts. I guess Nellie Tinkle thinks she's gettin' a dang car with all the ones she turned in. I tell y'all I had to have my husband, Dew, help me carry 'em all the way back over to our trailer on account of how heavy they was. Now that I think about it, I ought to make her pay for his doggone chiropractor bill since it was them doggone hints of hers that nearly threw him in the dang hospital! Who in the heck has that many doggone hints in the first place? What kind of freak is she? Ain't she got some kind of life? I tell you, I got a good mind to go over there and give her what for! Oh, wait a minute. She was the one who made me that fudge cake for my birthday, wasn't she? Oh, I forgot all about that. That was real good. I nearly ate the whole thing myself. Well, there ain't really nothin' wrong with that many hints, now is there. But don't think I actually found the dang time to type all them doggone things up and put 'em in this here book!

Go ahead and get out your marker one more time, so you can highlight your favorite hints out of all the ones the High Chaparral gang submitted that I chose to use.

## Hints Lot by Lot

- You can easily sharpen any pair of scissors by simply takin' a sheet of sandpaper and cuttin' it up into little pieces.
- A little petroleum jelly spread on your face and then massaged deep into the skin after a good face washin' will leave your face soft and gentle.
- We keep a powder puff in the flour so we can just use that when we got to put a little flour in a pan or on our rollin' pin.
- If you want to look years younger, put a little castor oil (the kind that don't smell) around your eyes when you go to bed. Wipe it off in the mornin'.
- When you put your trash out for the garbage collector, spray a little bit of ammonia on it to keep animals out of it.

—Opal Lamb-Inman, Lot #1
—Dick Inman, Lot #1
—Uri Krochichin, Lot #1
—Buck N. Hiney, Lot #1

- If you got unstained furniture, rather than buyin' that expensive stuff down at Lamb's, just make yourself a strong batch of unsweetened tea. Take a sponge and put a generous coat of tea on the furniture. Let dry and repeat to get a darker color finish.
- If you got a loose screw, just put a little nail polish in the hole and then rescrew the screw. When it dries it should hold good.
- Just before bakin', throw some salt on the bottom of your oven. This way if you have spills, the salt will help you clean the oven when you wipe it out.
- If you take a common wire hanger and run it through your blouse, slacks, or dress, it will get out the static electricity.
- If you apply a thin layer of wax to your ashtrays you can just quickly

dump 'em and give a fast wipe without havin' to wash 'em out every week.

—ANITA BIGGON, LOT #2

- If you find milk on sale, grab as much as you can afford and stick it in your freezer. Not only will it freeze, but it will last a good long time in that state.
- If you got those tough stains in your toilet, just add a can of that no-name soda pop, and let it set for an hour. Then just flush. If the stains still ain't gone, pop a top and try again.
- After you've boiled eggs, set the water aside and let it cool down to room temperature. Then pour it into your plants to give them all the good minerals and chemicals that the eggs give off. This will make your plants happy.
- If you want to cover up old nail holes in your panelin', simply rub toothpaste into the holes and then smooth 'em out with a damp sponge.
- You can get glue out of clothes, carpet, or upholstery by applyin' a vinegar-soaked rag to it.

—LOIS BUNCH, LOT #3
—HUBERT BUNCH, LOT #3

- Since Wendy moved in with me and C.M., I've found that the best way to keep the smell of my trailer fresh and enchantin' is to simply put a piece of foil on a cookie sheet, sprinkle on a teaspoon of cinnamon, and stick it in my stove, which I've preheated to 400 degrees F. If you leave the door open, within no time you'll have a happy-smellin' trailer home.
- When you get an unexpected spill on your carpet, quickly blot up as much of the liquid as you can, but remember to never rub the spot 'cause that will only spread it deeper into your carpet. Next, use some of your husband's shavin' cream that you've lathered up in your hand and apply to the carpet. Let it set for a minute, then wipe it up.
- You can take off that old built-up wax from your furniture by mixin' together ½ cup of water and ½ cup of vinegar and rubbin' it on with a cloth.
- You can clean your washin' machine by simply pourin' a gallon of distilled vinegar into the washer and runnin' it on a short cycle.

- A thin layer of floor wax on your clean windowsills will make 'em easy to clean in the future with just a damp sponge.

—C.M. Tinkle, Lot #4
—Nellie Tinkle, Lot #4
—Wendy Bottom, Lot #4

- Tired of them pesky bugs gettin' at your outside plants and such? Simply put an onion, 2 cloves of garlic, 1½ tablespoons of dishwashin' soap, and 2 cups of water in a blender and let them mix on high for a minute. Strain all the chunks out and pour it into one of your empty spray bottles. Spray the mixture on your plants, flowers, and other outside items. Repeat after a rainfall.
- When you have to open a can of tomato paste, make sure to open both ends. This way you can just easily push all the paste out at one time without havin' to try and scrape it out.
- A little car wax rubbed on clean plastic counterstops will make 'em shine like they was brand new.
- Your plants will love old lemonade that you're ready to throw out. So think of them first.
- When you've got to thread a needle, start off by sprayin' a little hair spray on your index finger and thumb. Then run the end of the thread across them. This should cause your thread to stiffen up long enough for you to get it through the eye of the needle.

—Momma Boxcar, Lot #5
—Daddy Boxcar, Lot #5

- Rinse out old milk jugs and fill 'em almost to the top with water. Put the lids back on and put 'em in your freezer. Then when you decide to use your ice chest, you can simply put one of the frozen jugs in there to keep everything cold, instead of wastin' good ice that could be used in drinks.
- A lazy Susan by your bed can come in real handy when you have several items that you want to get to without havin' to get out of bed.
- Since oil holds fragrances longer, add a little petroleum jelly to the areas of your body where you'll be sprayin' on the perfume.
- If you're like me, you've probably got sticky drawers. Well, that can be taken care of by simply rubbing a wax candle along the runners.

- Speakin' of sticky, if you have to replant a cactus, you can use your ice tongs to handle the little devil without worryin' about gettin' pricked.

—DONNA SUE BOXCAR, LOT #6

- When you get your first paycheck for the month, cash it and put $15 in quarters in a big mayonnaise jar. Every day when you get up, before you leave the trailer, take a minute to pray. Then when you leave, take out a quarter. And then at night, do the same. Say a prayer and take out a quarter. Then on the last Sunday of the month, whatever is left in the jar can be put in the offerin' plate as a special gift to God. Not only will this help you to remember to pray every day (grace at mealtimes don't count), but it'll also give you enough money to buy me a soda when we see each other.
- You can get those water rings out of any pulpit or piece of furniture by simply takin' a wet cloth and addin' a dab of toothpaste to it. Gently rub on the spot till it comes clean.
- If you find that you've run out of fabric softener right in the middle of a wash cycle, simply add 2 cups of white wine vinegar to the rinse cycle.
- You can avoid tangled up necklaces by screwin' cup hooks all along your closet and hangin' your pearls and assorted necklaces there.
- Got a crack in one of your favorite plates? Don't throw it away. Instead put it in a pan of boilin' sweet milk and let it boil for 45 minutes. It will be as good as new when you take it out.

—PASTOR IDA MAY BEE, LOT #7
—BROTHER WOODY BEE, LOT #7

- Empty film canisters are great for storin' your nose plugs when you're not swimmin'.
- If you go out to start your car and your locks are frozen over, just take a lighter to your key for a few seconds. This will heat up the key and you can then put it in the lock. Let it set for a few seconds and then softly turn. Just make sure you're not holdin' the key with your bare fingers or you will get burned.
- You can make your windows look good even in wintertime by addin' ½ cup of antifreeze to your window cleaner. Shake well and then clean as usual.

- If you heat your nail before hammerin' it into the wall, it will go in faster and won't hurt your walls. Again, just make sure that you don't hold the nail with your bare hand or you will get burned.
- If you want your tennis shoes to look nice and white like mine, add ½ cup of lemon juice to the rinse water. It won't do much for the smell, but they will look very nice and bright.

—LULU BELL BOXCAR, LOT #8

- I've found that addin' 3 tablespoons of bakin' soda to a cup of water and microwavin' it for 3 minutes makes the inside of the microwave a breeze to clean. And it smells much better than the old traditional vinegar way of cleanin' it out.
- Dip the bristles of your new broom into hot salt water before usin' it and it will last a lot longer.
- You can instantly kill those wild weeds or grasses that grow between the concrete with salted boiled water.
- Spilled candle wax in your carpet? Just put a brown paper sack on top of the wax and then add an iron set on medium on top of that. Let it set for a bit and take off the iron. The wax should now be melted onto the paper sack. Carefully lift off. If it doesn't always lift up, use ice on the wax. When it freezes you can simply break it off the carpet.
- If you have a recipe that calls for bread crumbs and you're all out, just crumble up unsweetened cereal and use that instead.

—JUANITA HIX, LOT #9
—HARLIND HIX, LOT #9

- Bug and spider problems? Just get a small bucket of hedge apples and put 'em in a corner. You won't see the critters again.
- The best way to whiten yellow teeth, or a single yellow tooth for that matter, is to dip your toothbrush in a mashed-up strawberry and brush.
- If you've got too much soap in your clothes washer, just add a little fabric softener.
- Bees and wasps don't mix with flamin' hair spray. You can, however, simply spray 'em with hair spray. This will make their wings stick together and they can now be carefully lifted up with a piece of paper and gently placed back outside.

- If you boil your darkened aluminum pans in a solution of 1 quart of water with 2 teaspoons of cream of tartar for 20 minutes, the brownish stain will vanish.

—OLLIE WHITE, LOT #10

- Throw those sour-smellin' sponges in a sink, add ⅓ cup of bakin' soda, and fill it halfway with hot water. Slightly mix everythin' together and let it set for an hour. The sponges will smell just like new.
- Mix a gallon of water and an ashtray full of half-smoked cigarette butts together. Let set for a few hours. Strain and pour the water into a spray bottle and use on all your plants and flowers. If applied after each rainfall, this will keep the bugs and fungus away. Just don't use it on your veggie garden.
- Dip your knife in cold water before cuttin' an egg and your boiled yolks won't crumble while you slice.
- When makin' your husband's sandwiches for the next afternoon, wrap 'em in lettuce then in foil. This will keep the sandwich fresh tastin' and he can discard the foil and lettuce before he eats the sandwich.
- When you get ready to dust next time, first make up a solution of 1 tablespoon of fabric softener and 4 tablespoons of water. Add your dustin' cloth to this solution and then just dust. This mixture will kill the static electricity so your house or store won't draw the dust to it.

—KITTY CHITWOOD, LOT #11
—KYLE CHITWOOD, LOT #11

- Keep your brown sugar in the freezer, and it will never get hard.
- If you have a clogged shower head, simply boil it in a mixture of 1 quart of water and 1 cup of vinegar for 20 minutes.
- If you live in a trailer park where you must shovel your sidewalk after a snowfall, pay someone else to do it. If there is no one to pay, then first give your shovel a quick spray down with nonstick aerosol spray. It will make your job a lot easier.
- If it's Friday and you have to make an avocado dip for church on Sunday, and your avocado isn't ripe yet, put it in a bowl, cover it completely with flour, and let it set out on the counter. Say a prayer and let the Lord work his wonders.

- If you only need half that avocado, put the pit back in before you cover it and put it in the fridge and the rest won't turn brown early.

—SISTER BERTHA, LOT #12

- The best way to a beautiful lawn is by feedin' it a good sprayin' of 1 quart of water mixed with 1 cup of Epsom salts and 1 cup of ammonia, which you've mixed together thoroughly. Do this once a week.
- You can stop a pesky zipper that won't stay zipped by sprayin' hair spray along the zipper's teeth. Just be careful of the fabric on the sides of the zipper.
- I keep a large safety pin by my kitchen sink so that when I do dishes I can put my rings on it and safety pin it to my blouse.
- You can get rid of rust spots around the trailer by simply pourin' some hydrogen peroxide on the spot and then sprinklin' on some cream of tartar. Let it set for an hour and then just wipe away.
- WD-40 works wonders when it comes to gettin' scuff marks off your floors.

—MICKEY RAY KAY, LOT #13
—CONNIE KAY, LOT #13
—WANDA KAY, LOT #13

- If you store your candles in your freezer, they'll last longer when you light 'em.
- A cup of vinegar in your mop water will make your floor sparkle.
- Clean your thermos by fillin' it up with water and then droppin' in a denture-cleanin' tablet. Let it set for an hour and a half and then rinse it out.
- A light layer of floor wax on your ceilin' fan blades will make dustin' 'em later a breeze.
- You can avoid soap scum build-up in your shower by applyin' car wax to your walls. Buff them and get ready for a trouble-free shower.

—DOTTIE LAMB, LOT #14
—BEN BEAVER, LOT #14

- If you put a little touch of clear finger nail polish on each button of your shirt, the strings will almost never get frail and cause the buttons to fall off, unless of course you happen to put on weight and pop 'em across the room.

- If you find that your favorite shade of lipstick has melted, just put it in the freezer, and in no time you'll be able to use it again.
- You can use those old dryer sheets as furniture dusters. They are great!
- If you put a few sugar cubes in the same container that you keep your cheese, you will find that the cheese lasts longer without turnin' moldy.
- Forget those real pretty ironin' board covers. You can cut your ironin' time in half if you simply line your ironin' board with foil and cover this with a soft thin fabric cover. This way when you iron, the heat will reflect off of the foil and get the wrinkles out a lot faster and with less effort.

—DONNY OWENS, LOT #15
—KENNY LYNN, LOT #15

- Puttin' a shot of vodka in your vase water will make any fresh flowers you get from a gentleman admirer or your son last longer. Plus, if you run short on booze one night you can always drink the flower water.
- You can clean a mildewed shower curtain by washin' it with a normal load's worth of laundry detergent and a bit of bicarbonate of soda. Then let it set in a solution of salt water and the juice of 2 lemons for an hour. Hang up the curtain and let it drip dry.
- Save those old empty paper towel rolls to store extension cords in.
- Coffee filters make great, expensive-lookin' napkins when you got important people over for dinner or just a nip.
- I like to wash out my plastic sandwich bags and keep 'em in the freezer before I use 'em again. This helps to keep out the mildew.

—MOMMA BALLZAK, LOT #16

- Keep your old dryer sheets to use as protective stuffin' for when you have to pack somethin' in a box.
- Add a pinch of salt to your coffee basket before you make the coffee for the best coffee you've ever had.
- Once every few months, take a paper bag and put in a cup of salt. Add some of your plastic flowers and shake. Keep addin' the flow-

ers and shakin'. Change the salt after four or five bouquets' worth of flowers. You'll be amazed at how well this cleans the flowers.
- When you get a new pair of panty hose, wash 'em first, then put 'em in a pot with 1 gallon of water and 2 cups of salt. Let 'em soak for 3 to 4 hours. Rinse in cold water and drip-dry. This will help make your panty hose last longer.
- Take a fresh dryer sheet and put it in an envelope. Put it in your car's glove box or under your seat for an inexpensive car freshener.

—Faye Faye LaRue, Lot #17
—Tina Faye Stopenblotter, Lot #17

- A few cotton balls soaked in vanilla extract and put in an old disposable pot pie pan will keep your fridge smellin' good year-round.
- Take a pot of warm water and add 3 tablespoons of bleach and 3 tablespoons of bakin' soda. Add your hairbrushes, hair clips, bobby pins, curlers, and combs and stir 'em around to clean 'em, then rinse. Set the items out to dry.
- When you've used a lipstick all the way down to the end of the tube, scrape out what is left and mix it with a little petroleum jelly to make a great lip gloss.
- To avoid fogged-up bathroom mirrors, smear a light layer of shavin' cream on the window, then wipe it off. No fog!
- If you put all your socks in a pillowcase, tie the top into a knot, and throw it in the washer, you can wash socks without ever havin' to worry about losin' another sock in the washer again.

—Ruby Ann Boxcar, Lot #18
—Dew Ballzak, Lot #18

- When lookin' for a lost contact lens, use a piece of bread to feel around on the floor. The contact lens will stick to the bread, which won't scratch it.
- Pour any leftover coffee or sweet tea into an ice tray so that when you want a glass, and you don't feel like makin' a pitcher or a pot, you can just grab a few cubes, stick 'em in a glass or cup, and melt 'em down in your microwave. If it's tea you're nukin', just add a few more regular ice cubes to get it back to the right temperature.
- You can take care of them car scratches by takin' a wax crayon of the same color to 'em.

- You can get heavily soiled clothes clean by addin' ½ cup of ammonia to your wash water.
- If you got to keep your freezer outside in your shed or garage, spray it down with furniture polish and it won't rust on you.

—VANCE POOL, LOT #19
—HARRY LOMBARDI, LOT #19
—ELROY DASAFE, LOT #19

- To keep your hands young and fresh like mine, add 2 teaspoons of bakin' soda to your dishwater. Not only will it make your hands soft, but it'll also help you cut through all that grease.
- When mixed with a little water to make a paste, leftover grits and oatmeal make for a great facial.
- When you're in a hurry and you've just painted your nails, you can get 'em to dry in half the time by stickin' 'em in a freezer or just sprayin' 'em down with a nonstick aerosol cookin' spray.
- You can clean up spilled red wine from the carpet by simply pourin' a little white wine directly on the stain. Leave it there to do its work. Then wipe it up.
- Avoid leanin' on furniture with rollers.

—LITTLE LINDA, LOT #20

# Ask Ruby Ann . . .

Dear Ruby Ann,

I'm so excited to talk to you. My husband and I have been married for three months and we've just managed to get our very first trailer home. And the good news is that we were able to steal it away for less than $300 at a police auction. I don't know what it was used for, but it is a 2001 model. We were just thrilled! We found a lot to park it on and are cleanin' it up from top to bottom. We've managed to get the red-splattered stains off the walls, but we had to pull most of the carpet because those stains and the chalk marks just wouldn't come up. The only problem we seem to be having is with the odor that is in the trailer. It smells like someone has died in it. Well, maybe it's not quite that bad, but we would like to get rid of it. Can you help?

Also, if you could only give one helpful hint to a newly married couple like me and my husband who are movin' into their very first trailer home, what would it be?

We are so happy to be trailer park people and we love your books.

Tim and Shannon
Hays, Kansas

Dear Tim and Shannon,

Wow, what a deal y'all got. I'm so happy for y'all as well. Welcome to my world. Hey, as far as that smell goes, don't worry about it. Twice a year the state makes us hose down my sister's trailer, so I know what true stench is, and yours can't be that bad. But this year we tried somethin' a little different, and it sure got rid of that smell fast. You combine 2 cups of your favorite fabric softener with 2 cups of bakin' soda, and 4 cups of warm water. Stir it up real good and put it in a spray bottle. Take this stuff and spray it on your walls, floors, carpets, curtains, cellin's, and every place else you can find in your trailer. If this doesn't do the trick, then I'd suggest you take everythin' out of the trailer that ain't nailed down, drive it over to the nearest car wash, and give that son of a gun a good high-pressure power spray from top to bottom. But try the spray stuff first. Here's the recipe.

Makes 6 cups' worth

4 cups very warm water
2 cups bakin' soda
2 cups fabric softener
1 average-size clean empty spray bottle

Pour all the ingredients into the bottle. Put the lid on and shake the bottle real good to mix the ingredients. You want to make sure that the bakin' soda dissolves completely before usin' it. And just reshake before each use.

As far as the one helpful hint goes, if you was livin' anywhere close to me, I'd have to lovin' tell y'all that you should go ahead and have your tubes tied. After all, the last thing anybody in this world needs is more little ones runnin' through our yards like a pack of wild cows on a feedin' frenzy, knockin' over lawn furniture and tippin' over our little yard statues. Who needs it? No, go ahead and get them tubes tied and just go with dogs. Not only are they sweet and lovin', but if they get in your yard and pee, it ain't in your birdbath or under your trailer after rippin' off a loose piece of your "realistic rock" skirtin'.

Welcome aboard, neighbor.

Love, Kisses, and Trailer Park Wishes,
Ruby Ann Boxcar

# Epilog: Afterthoughts . . . I Think

I'm sure that as you read through this book, page-by-page, you might have come across some things that you already do in your everyday life. Why, I know that I got some of my ideas on life from my momma and daddy, just like most of y'all have picked up traits or ways of doin' things from your folks. The only difference is that while y'all realize more and more each day that you're becomin' your parents, I've gone in the opposite direction from my folks, and have become a star.

Of course we all can't be international celebrities, which is one of the reasons that I've taken the time to share my ways of livin' real good with y'all, so that regardless of what kind of life you live, you can still have them starlike qualities in your own home if you just follow the advice I've given in this book. As a matter of fact, you might want to do what I've done to keep me in that state of mind. You know how when you're dietin', you put one of your fat pictures up on the fridge, which in my case is any photo I've ever taken since birth, if you know what I mean. For some reason that seems to help us to remember that we can't keep eatin' like we do or we'll keep lookin' like we do in that photo that you got underneath a magnet. And as you know, it works pretty good for about the first two days and then you've ripped that picture into tiny little pieces and thrown it into the trash can along with that extra large pizza box and pint-size container of strawberry cheesecake ice cream, which you've just consumed in record time. But for a while it does make you feel like you can drop those ten or two-hundred pounds. Well, I've taken that same idea and used it for makin' me feel good each day. What I've done is take a piece of cardboard and cut out a great big star. I've wrapped foil around it and hung it on my bedroom door so regardless of what I'm doin' I'll always be reminded that I'm a star. Why, I've even got a second duplicate star hangin' on the back of my bedroom door, so that whenever I wake up and start out that door to begin my day, I'm instantly reminded that I'm still a star. And even at night, with the slightest moonlight in the sky, that foil picks it up so one of the last things I see as I lay in bed is that star of mine. I even used to hang a star up on the bathroom door so that when I went to bathe every day, which I do by the way, I'd recall that I'm someone special—a star. Of course after one of the days I was stuck with my Me-Ma on account of some stupidness goin' on down at the Last Stop Nursing Home, I took the bathroom star down after she mistakenly went into the wrong room after wakin' up from a nap on the couch. But that's not important.

If y'all take the time to make your own foil stars, then you can also enjoy the same special feelin's that I do. Just think of how this will change your life. You open that electric or gas bill, knowin' full well that you can't pay it, but instead of worryin' about it, you just look at your bedroom door and know that it don't matter, 'cause you're a star! Oh, when they come to disconnect your cable 'cause y'all ordered all them pay-per-view wrestlin' specials last month knowin' full well that you couldn't afford 'em, you just look at your bedroom door and know that it don't matter 'cause you're a star! And as you're led out your front door in handcuffs for thousands of dollars in bad checks, you quickly take one last look at your bedroom door and know that it don't matter 'cause *you're a star!*

And one last thing in closin'. I know that some of y'all ain't crafty, and that if I come into your homes after you've read this book and put it to practice in your daily livin' I'm gonna find some absolute pieces of junk settin' on your tables or suspended from your ceilin's. But you know what? That's okay. If you like it, if you are excited 'cause you made it with your own hands, then display it. And don't let anyone's opinions, regardless of how right on the money they might otherwise be, convince you to take it down. After all, the number-one rule to livin' real good is, "I do things that make me happy each and every day without hurtin' anyone or anything on purpose or unintentionally." So please, just enjoy life to its fullest and live each day with rule number one deeply implanted in your thoughts. Oh, and don't forget to practice rule number two as well, which is, "If at anytime in your life someone with a real painful look on their face points to somethin' that you've either made, cooked, or put on, and asks if you got that idea from Ruby Ann Boxcar, deny it to your dyin' day."

Love, Kisses, and Trailer Park Wishes,
Ruby Ann Boxcar

# Acknowledgments

Thanks once again to the whole gang at Citadel Press/ Kensington Publishing for always makin' my writin's look as top-notch as I do. I also have to give a big thank you to my assistant, Kevin Wiley, who not only helped me construct some of these crafts on account of my busy schedule, but who has been able to help me maintain the high-fashion look that has become both my trademark as well as a goal for those in life to try to achieve the highest that they can. And if it wasn't for his company, Wiley Designs, who've managed to put my essence in both the clothin' they make for me as well as the purses and jewelry that I sport every day of the year, I'd still be buyin' my clothes down at the There She Blows Fashion Boutique. What would an acknowledgment section be without a thank you to my older sister, Donna Sue, who makes me realize every time I smell her whisky-scotch-bourbon-vodka-gin-rum-tequila-Aqua-Velva-rich breath that it's important to follow your dreams, and wear a good bra with everything regardless if the straps show or not. A special thanks to my musical director Robert for makin' me reach for them high notes even when my dogs are howlin'. I also want to thank my sister's choreographer, Curtis, for finally acceptin' the fact that I'm a happily married woman, and keepin' his hands to himself. I got to thank all the folks at the High Chaparral Trailer Park, me and my husband's friends and family, the people at the TV stations who put me on and in the media who print stories about me, and the literary escorts and hotel employees that make each one of my city visits special. And in closin' let me thank the three powers that make these books of mine possible; God, the bookstore employees that suggest my works to their customers, and last but not least, all my fans who come out to see me at the bookstores, buy my books, and write me e-mails or sign my guest book at www.rubyannboxcar.com. Thanks, y'all.

# Index

# Coming in 2004

She showed us how to add spice to your meals in *Ruby Ann's Down Home Trailer Park Cookbook;* she showed us how to celebrate all of the important days of the year in *Ruby Ann's Down Home Trailer Park Holiday Cookbook;* she showed us how to use our grills to their highest level of potential in *Ruby Ann's Down Home Trailer Park BBQin' Cookbook;* she even showed us the joys of life right here in *Ruby Ann's Down Home Trailer Park Guide to Livin' Real Good*—but coming in May of 2004, the queen of the double-wide world will be showing us the true meaning of life as she answers your personal letters in *Dear Ruby Ann: Down Home Advice About Lovin', Livin', and the Whole Shebang.* Just when you thought it was safe to close Donna Sue's bartending guide and come out from behind the cocktail napkins and stir straws, Ruby Ann hits you with yet another socially relevant volume from the "down home" series. But this time she's taken your dirty laundry, private problems, and in some cases, thought-provoking questions, and she's answered them usin' the kind of thought processes and heartfelt compassion that has made her the humble philosopher and guru adviser to the world that she is today. As Ruby Ann shows us in this next release, no problem is too big and no answer is too over the top. For example, when a troubled mom seeks advice on what she can do to stop her little child from inappropriately peeing in the bathwater during tub-time, it is the quick mind of Ruby Ann that comes up with the unique answer of feeding the little one a half pound of Velveta cheese thirty minutes before it's time to take a bath. But don't think that Ruby Ann stops at just childrearing. No, this big-haired blue-eye-shadow-wearing counselor to the troubled also answers your dilemmas on family, friends, neighbors, drunks, smokers, and even bail bondsmen. Ruby Ann tells us what we can do when we have those friends, police, government officials, or just plain old escaped relatives stopping by for an unexpected visit or overnight stay. This diva of the cat-eyed glasses tells us how to handle sexual harassment at work, a handle sexual harassment at work, a shopaholic wife, and travelin' with in-laws. No question is too difficult as we find out when a reader asks her if it's okay for him to wear a T-shirt and swim trunks for his upcoming adult baptism. And no topic is too bold, as we can clearly see when she tells a woman who is hosting a Tupperware party to inform her guests to bring a big appetite with them, but yet not to serve any food until they've bought enough items for "you to get a real good hostess gift." As the title implies, Ms. Boxcar also tackles matters of the heart, dealin' with people who don't own an Elvis record or movie, both men and women who should only put on a pair of white pants if the screen won't work at a family slide-show gatherin', and the rest of the world.

And if all that wasn't enough, Ruby Ann spills the beans on the gang at the High Chaparral Trailer Park. You won't believe the tales she tells on her fellow trailer park dwellers and what they've been up to: Did Opal Lamb-Inman really dump Dick? Has Tina Faye Stopenblotter found love? Is Faye Faye LaRue really using her psychic abilities to help out her neighbors? How is Donna Sue's Wienies on Wheels hot dog business doing? Did Sister Bertha and Pastor Ida actually have a falling out and is Sister Bertha starting her own church? Are Dottie Lamb and the manager of the trailer park Ben Beaver finally hearing wedding bells, or is that just someone at the door?

Everything is revealed and all questions are answered in May 2004, when the newest release from the madcap mind of Ruby Ann Boxcar, *Dear Ruby Ann: Down Home Advice About Lovin', Livin', and the Whole Shebang,* hits bookstores nationwide.